DATE DUE

LATINO SUCCESS

Insights from 100 of America's Most Powerful Latino Business Professionals

Augusto A. Failde
and William S. Doyle

SIMON & SCHUSTER

SIMON & SCHUSTER
Rockefeller Center
1230 Avenue of the Americas
New York, NY 10020

Copyright © 1996 by Augusto A. Failde and William S. Doyle
All rights reserved,
including the right of reproduction
in whole or in part in any form.

SIMON & SCHUSTER and colophon are registered trademarks
of Simon & Schuster Inc.

Designed by Irving Perkins Associates

Manufactured in the United States of America
10 9 8 7 6 5 4 3 2 1

Library of Congress Cataloging-in-Publication Data
Failde, Augusto A.
    Latin success : insights from America's most powerful
Latino business executives / Augusto A. Failde and
William S. Doyle.
        p.   cm.
    Includes index.
    1. Success in business—United States.   2. Hispanic
Americans in business.   3. Hispanic American business
enterprises—Management.
    I. Doyle, William, date.   II. Title.
HF5386.F227   1996
650.1'089'68073—dc20   96-920
                                                    CIP
ISBN 0-684-81312-2

Excerpts from "Education of the Heart, César E. Chávez, In
His Own Words," used by permission of the César E. Chávez
Foundation, P.O. Box 62, Keene, California 93531

ACKNOWLEDGMENTS

We are most grateful to the scores of Latino professionals, entrepreneurs, and executives around the country who took time out from their busy schedules to share their insights with us. They are the real face of Latino success in America today. Our only regret is that we couldn't include more of them in the book.

In life there are people who "get it" and people who don't. Our editor at Simon & Schuster, Fred Hills, "got" this project so quickly that we're convinced he must have been Latino in another life. We thank Fred and Carolyn Reidy, President of the Trade Division of Simon & Schuster, for championing our book and helping make this journey possible.

We also thank our agent, Mel Berger of the William Morris Agency in New York, and Padre Biglin, Walmer Bravo, Joe and Maria Kennedy, Ralph Paniagua, Naomi Moriyama, Lily Numeyer, Vita Morales, Ed, David, and Pam at Coudert Brothers, and Caroline Downing of A Steno Service.

We dedicate this book to:

Cristina García-Montes (1959–1992), "who listened when no one would,"

our families: Papa Mendicoa, Ninetta, Aland, Juancy, Arlene, Ortelio, Gisela, Gelcy, Bill, Marilou, and Kate,

and the millions of Latino and Latina professionals—teachers, doctors, engineers, construction workers, housewives, police officers, entrepreneurs and executives, students, parents, and grandparents—who are transforming America.

CONTENTS

INTRODUCTION

FOR as long as I can remember, my parents have tried to help me understand the lessons of life through *dichos*—sayings passed down through the generations. One of them, *"Los niños y los locos siempre te diran la verdad"*—Children and the mentally ill will always tell you the truth, explains how this book came about.

One afternoon not long ago, I took my twelve-year-old brother Aland to see the movie *The Fugitive*. Earlier that day, Aland and my parents had had a spirited debate about the need for him to master Spanish as well as English, not only to communicate with them, but to stay connected to his heritage and equip him with a language skill that would be a real asset for the future.

"Yeah, so why should I learn Spanish?" Aland said as we came out of the theater. "The only guys who spoke Spanish in the movie were a janitor and a prisoner." He was right. His comment bothered me quite a bit, so I decided to try to find some books for him about successful Latinos in the United States.

A few weeks later I ran into my friend Bill Doyle at the food pantry in Times Square where we both do volunteer work. Bill knows Aland and agreed to help me look for some books for him. We began searching around bookstores in

New York. We looked. And looked. Everywhere. We found nothing.

A few weeks later, I sat down to watch one of my favorite TV shows, *Ellen*. The episode began with the introduction of a new character, a Latina. I thought, "Great! A Latina on prime time!" My excitement soon collapsed into disgust and anger. Despite the very few Latino characters on TV and a social climate of supposed cultural sensitivity and "political correctness," the show managed to combine at least six stereotypes into a single character:

- a Latina who can't speak English
- a Latina who is a "loose and easy" woman
- a Latina who is an illegal immigrant
- a Latina who is an extortionist
- a Latina who is smuggling her numerous children across the border
- a Latina who can't be trusted

The show was just the latest in a long line of insulting media images of Latinos in the United States. In fact, positive images of Latinos in mainstream American media are almost nonexistent. The few times we do appear, we're all too often portrayed as killers, convicts, dope dealers, gang lords, prostitutes, and illegal immigrants. According to a recent study by the Center for Media and Public Affairs for the National Council of La Raza:

- Hispanics account for only 1 percent of network TV prime-time characters
- Hispanics are portrayed on TV in negative and violent roles more than twice as often as blacks and whites
- Hispanics are four times more likely to commit a crime on TV than either blacks or whites

My phone rang. It was Bill, who was watching the same show. We both couldn't believe what we were seeing. By the end of the call, we decided to try to produce a book that would showcase what the media rarely shows us—the experiences and insights of the scores of highly successful Latino men and women who are making huge contributions to this country.

===

THE LATINO EXPLOSION

The ascendancy of Hispanic residents of the United States represents their reemergence as the dominant minority in America after more than 400 years, decades before English colonists landed at Jamestown, Virginia.

The New York Times, October 9, 1994

RIGHT now, across the United States, something remarkable is happening.* From Miami to L.A., from New York to Houston, from Chicago to Dallas, San Diego, Phoenix, and a thousand places in between, millions of Latinos are riding a wave of business and cultural expansion that will accelerate through the 1990s and beyond.

- *There are 28 million Latinos in the United States,* representing more than 10 percent of the population and $220 billion in purchasing power. Latino purchasing power will more than double in the next six years.
- *The Latino population is growing eight times faster than the non-Latino population.* By 2000, the Latino population will grow to 34 million and will become the biggest minority by 2010, when Latinos will number 42 million.
- *Latino-owned businesses grew from 250,000 in 1987 to 720,000 in 1995.*

- *Many Latinos are bilingual and bicultural,* combining strong ethnic pride with a strong desire to succeed in the mainstream American culture. While many Latinos live in bilingual households and choose to speak Spanish at home, the majority of Latinos can speak English.

- *In mid-1994,* The Wall Street Journal *reported the emergence of "Latino America,"* an entirely new demographic segment concentrated in New York, Miami, Chicago, and the Southwest that represents a "giant step in achievement" and is "college-bound and moving up."

---

*SOURCES:

U.S. Census Bureau
Aspen Institute, 1990, "Handsome Dividends: A Handbook to Demystify the U.S. Hispanic Markets"
SRC 1991 Market Study
DRI-McGraw Hill, "The Use of Spanish in the Home: Analysis and Forecast to 2010," September 1993
1994 Univision McGraw-Hill Study
Hispanic magazine, July 1994
Hispanic Business, April 1994, December 1995
Advertising Age, January 24, 1994
The Wall Street Journal, July 21, 1994
Jose Adan Trevino, Chairman of the Board, United States Hispanic Chamber of Commerce, press conference, June 9, 1995

THE PANEL OF LATINO BUSINESS PROFESSIONALS

AT the vanguard of this blossoming "cultural revolution" is the face of Latino America rarely seen in the media: the millions of Latino professionals who are transforming the face of America. But while many of us and our children will compete in the business world, our exposure and access to successful Latino and Latina professionals is often very limited. They are an untapped and priceless source of practical advice about success in America.

We conducted in-depth interviews with a panel of one

hundred of America's most successful Latino business executives and entrepreneurs. Their insights are reflected in the pages that follow, and most of them are quoted by name.

They were identified from sources including *Who's Who Among Hispanic Americans, Hispanic Business, Hispanic* magazine, *The Wall Street Journal, Fortune, Business Week,* and *Forbes,* and by referrals from the panelists themselves. The panel includes Latino executives and entrepreneurs from the *Hispanic Business* Corporate Elite and 500 Largest Hispanic-Owned Businesses Reports and *Fortune*'s 500 Largest Industrial Companies and 100 Fastest-Growing Companies.

Some of the panelists have advanced degrees. Many do not. The panel represents a wide cross section of Latinos, people who trace their heritage from Mexico, Puerto Rico, Cuba, the Dominican Republic, Central and South America, Africa, and Spain. They come from families who have been in this country for ten generations and families who only recently came to the United States.

They are residents of New York, Los Angeles, Miami, Texas, Arizona, Chicago, San Francisco, San Diego, Denver, New Jersey, Boston, Kansas City, Ohio, and a number of other cities and states in the Northeast, Midwest, South, Sunbelt, and California.

They are corporate CEOs, presidents, executive and senior vice presidents, managing directors, vice presidents, and small business owners. They work for companies like Reebok, AT&T, McDonald's, Ford, CBS, Seagram, Citibank, Motorola, American Express, Colgate, Nestlé, and the country's hottest Hispanic-owned businesses.

Over the course of a year, we visited with them in their offices and boardrooms, on factory floors and over the telephone. We asked them:

- What are the most crucial *success insights* you've learned?
- What have been the *biggest surprises* of your career?

- What insights have you discovered in the areas of
  —*managing people:* bosses, clients, mentors
  —*managing yourself:* goals, mistakes and failures?
- Who are the *best and worst bosses* you've ever had—what lessons did you learn?
- What was the *best day of your career?* How about *the worst?* What did you learn?
- What *insights and experiences* have you had that are of special interest "for Latinos only"?

What We Found

We often hear how Latinos in the United States are so different from each other: "Mexicans are very different from Cubans," "Puerto Ricans are very different from Mexicans," and so on. But while we do come from a multitude of cultures and experiences, our interviews revealed a great many commonalities: the values we share, pride in our heritage and language assets, ambition for the success of our families, and the shared experience of pursuing "the American Dream."

We asked our panelists to be very candid, to open up and share their lessons from the heart about the challenges, failures, frustrations, victories, and triumphs of succeeding as a Latino in America today. But we were at times amazed by their emotional candor, particularly when they spoke about the racism and prejudice they have encountered, remarks we have included in sections throughout the book labeled "Off the Record," in which the speakers are not identified by name to preserve their anonymity.

Brief biographies of our panel members appear when their remarks are first quoted (an index to these biographies appears at the end of the book). Where additional remarks by the same panel member appear elsewhere in the book, the person is identified only by name, title, and affiliation.

Frankly, as with any group as diverse as this, they don't always agree with each other. In fact, you may at times not agree with them either. Over the course of the interviews, however, one major message came through over and over, loud and clear, from nearly everyone we spoke with:

The strengths and values that most make us Latino—family, pride, courage, passion, compassion, language assets, loyalty, cultural sensitivity, adaptability—are precisely the same strengths and values that are the keys to success in America today.

We have broken this message down into seven major "Latino Success Insights":

LATINO SUCCESS INSIGHTS

Insight 1. **L**evel the Playing Field

Insight 2. **A**dvice

Insight 3. **T**remendous Asset

Insight 4. **I**mage

Insight 5. **N**ever Fear Failure

Insight 6. *Orgullo* (Pride)

Insight 7. **S**tay on Track

These insights, which we have used as titles for the sections of the book that follow, summarize both individually and collectively the ways in which our panel of Latino business executives got where they are today—and what they learned along the way. These are real-life stories, struggles, and triumphs of people who have taken different paths to success, but learned many of the same lessons.

We hope their wisdom will provide help in your own journey, and a reminder that the faces of success in America are our own.

And finally, we believe that readers will find the resource section at the end of this book especially useful. Based on a national survey of executives nationwide, conducted by *Hispanic* magazine, it lists the 100 companies that offer the greatest career opportunities for Latinos.

WHEN my family and I came to this country, we had to leave everything behind. Back in Havana, our family photographs hung on the walls. Our wedding gifts sat on the shelves. Every material property we owned . . . overnight became government property.

But amid that turmoil, two treasured possessions remained mine because they simply could not be taken away by the newly arrived Cuban rulers.

Firstly, even though I had to leave behind my diploma from Yale . . . and even though I had to leave behind the specially engraved dictionary I earned as valedictorian of my high school graduating class . . . I carried with me, safely in my head, the meaning of that diploma and of that dictionary.

I still had my education.

And secondly, even though the Havana Coca-Cola bottling plant where I had worked was to be confiscated, I still had a job. And it wasn't just any job. It was a job with The Coca-Cola Company.

From that point on—as you might guess—the story improves significantly. And that story—*my* story—boils down to a single, inspiring reality . . . the reality that a young immigrant could come to this country, be given a chance to work hard and apply his skills, and ultimately earn the opportunity to lead not only a large corporation, but an institution that actually symbolizes the very essence of America and American ideals.

Roberto C. Goizueta
Chairman and CEO, The Coca-Cola Company

From keynote address at Independence Day Ceremonies at Thomas Jefferson Home, Monticello, Virginia, July 4, 1995. After speaking, Mr. Goizueta joined sixty-seven new Americans on the west lawn. As they took the oath of citizenship, he stood with them and restated his own oath of citizenship as an American.

We cannot seek achievement for ourselves and forget about progress and prosperity for our community. . . . Our ambitions must be broad enough to include the aspirations and needs of others, for their sakes and our own.

César E. Chávez
(1927–1993)
Founder, United Farm Workers of America, AFL-CIO

Be proud of who you are, be proud of your culture, of your language. . . . You will do well and you will mix beautifully in both cultures and in any culture in the world.

Lionel Sosa, Chairman, DMB&B Américas

INSIGHT 1

LEVEL THE PLAYING FIELD

For Latinos, education, communication, and performance are the great "levelers."

Education is becoming the great equalizer that cuts across gender, color, religion, and national origin.

Eduardo Aguirre
Senior Vice President and Division Executive
NationsBank

HISPANICS are still sadly underrepresented in corporate boardrooms, in the executive suites, and in the partner ranks of most professions across the United States. This is beginning to change.

There are many problems facing the Hispanic community: unemployment and underemployment, an unacceptable high school dropout rate, limited access to economic advantages, discrimination, glass ceilings, crime, drugs, teen gangs, and other real and perceived obstacles.

Education is the most important thing that we need as Hispanics.

Several years ago I had the good fortune to come to know one of the recipients of our Go Tejano scholarship program. I'll call her Helen. She never knew her father and rarely saw her mother. She was raised by her *abuelita* on Social Security and welfare. She moved from relative to relative and school to school until her grandmother died when she was a junior in high school. She held down a part-time job with no means of transportation.

Still, with all these obstacles, Helen never wavered from her burning desire to go to college, and when her high school guidance counselors didn't select her to be interviewed by the Go Tejano scholarship committee, she didn't let that stop her. She went straight to them. She got the $2,000 scholarship from the Go Tejano committee, plus $11,000 from other scholarship sources.

Helen graduated from high school with a 4.0 grade point average. She is the first in her family to graduate from high school and the only one to go on to college. When I last saw her, she was a junior at the University of Houston majoring in hotel and restaurant management.

She told us she wants to come back to the Hispanic community and help others like her realize their dreams.

Those who are educated will get the best jobs. Those who aren't will get lesser jobs, suffer through unemployment, or be forced to scrape by on subsistence wages.

I come from a working family. I came here when I was fifteen years old, without my parents, with no knowledge of the English language. For several years, I was cared for, fed, and taught through the generosity of Catholic Charities and the United Way.

> *We must never forget where we've been if we are to master the future. We will achieve success only when we help these kids with so many dreams and so much determination achieve their own success.*

Eduardo Aguirre is Senior Vice President and Division Executive of NationsBank, the third largest banking organization in the United States. He is based in Houston. He graduated from Louisiana State University and joined a predecessor company of NationsBank as a vice president in 1977. He currently manages $2.5 billion in assets for the bank and was appointed by Governor George W. Bush to the Board of Regents of the University of Houston.

Have the street smarts to recognize your weaknesses and strengths. If you always play on your strengths and try to improve your weaknesses, you'll succeed. You don't have to be a genius.

Enrique Falla
Executive Vice President
Chief Financial Officer
Dow Chemical Company

STANDARDIZED test scores are only an indication of areas that you need to concentrate on and to improve on. They should not be a reading on your future. They don't determine where you're going to be. They're only helping you ID areas where you need to spend some more time.

I've seen an almost perfect correlation between IQ and the ability to get to the top: people who have an extremely high IQ will never make it to the top in management.

There's a big difference between being smart and being purely intelligent. I always say I'll take smart people before purely intelligent people.

People who are super-intelligent often think they know it all, and they don't deal with people well. They tend to be eccentric. Look at the top people in government and corporations and you'll see they aren't the ones with 180 IQs. You'll see them in the research lab, you'll see them in areas of a very narrow field of expertise, where personal interaction and leadership qualities are not paramount to their success. Einstein ran one heck of a research lab, but he could not have run a company.

What you need is commitment and hard work and you will succeed. As you go along your career and you have a series of successes, you will become very confident in your abilities.

Confidence is very, very powerful, provided that, in the process, you accept and recognize that you're not God, that you do have weaknesses and that you need to constantly work on your weaknesses and deficiencies.

Enrique C. Falla is Executive Vice President and Chief Financial Officer of Dow Chemical Company, a Fortune 500 company based in Midland, Michigan. He has been on the Dow board of directors since 1985, and also serves on the board of directors of K-Mart Corporation.

Education: we need that success on paper.

Christy Haubegger
Publisher
Latina Magazine

WE need educational credentials on paper. Some groups have a better opportunity to bootstrap themselves up through the "old boys' network." If you don't have a network, you'd better have everything else on paper, because that gives you legitimacy.

I know it's not fair, but it does get you in the door, and you need every open door you can get. School is a fantastic part of your network. I have a law degree from a good school, and the best thing about that is it makes people think I'm smart. That's not something that everybody else has to prove. Education is first and foremost about learning. But the connections and credentials it gives you are equally important.

Christy Haubegger is the Publisher of Latina Magazine in New York City. She is a Mexican-American who grew up in an adoptive home in Texas. She received her bachelor's degree from the University of Texas at Austin and her law degree from Stanford Law School. Latina Magazine, which she founded, is scheduled to launch nationally in 1996.

═══════════════

*For Hispanics, education is the best way to level
the playing field.*

Celeste De Armas
Senior Vice President and General Manager
Nestlé Refrigerated Food Company

I'M the only one of three kids to finish college. My parents
were always supportive of my educational interests but because they were not educated in this country, they could not
provide as much guidance as they would have liked. As a result, I was not as focused during my undergraduate years as
I should have been.

I realized business was my true calling in my junior year
in college. Prior to that, I had no real understanding of careers in business. My father worked in a technical field in
the film industry. My mother worked part-time in retail, but
not really a career per se. So within my own sphere of influence, business was just not something that I knew a lot
about or had a lot of contact with.

After graduation, I applied to business schools—most of
them out of state. I was in my early twenties, single, and living at home. For my parents and perhaps most first-
generation Hispanics, the concept of their single daughters
moving far from home to attend school was somewhat dis-
turbing. But getting my MBA away from home turned out
to be the very best thing I could have done, both personally
and professionally. Education is number one and most important. That for me was the thing that really opened the
doors for me career-wise. I don't know what I would be
doing today if I had not gotten that MBA. It gave me the opportunity to be on a level playing field with people who had
more of a silver spoon kind of upbringing.

Celeste De Armas is Senior Vice President and General Manager of
Nestlé Refrigerated Food Company in Solon, Ohio. She received a

bachelor's degree from Indiana University and began her career with
General Mills as a product manager.

═══════════════════

*Take one of the positions where you can stand
out. Your ability to impact the P&L, that's your
ability to stand out. You're not going to stay in a
back room.*

Jose Collazo
Chairman and President
Infonet

I was born in Puerto Rico and lived there through junior
high school. I've been with this company for twenty-six
years.

I joined Computer Sciences Corporation in 1969. They
started a new venture called Infonet. The idea was to allow
people to interconnect with a computer using terminals. It's
very common today, but back in 1969 it was very high-tech.

This company has always been a high-growth company.
Whether you were Latino or not really did not matter, it
wasn't even a factor. It was a start-up company growing very
fast, and I went from manager of scientific applications to
manager of commercial applications, to manager of both,
to director of industry planning, then director of marketing
planning, all in the span of maybe three years, because
we're a very fast-growing business.

At one point the chairman of CSC asked me if I would be
interested in going to Italy, because they just bought a company in Italy and they needed somebody who spoke Italian.
I said, "I don't speak Italian." He said, "Well, with a name
like yours, I figured you could learn it." I said, "Well, okay, I
can learn it." So I went to Italy.

I'm a classic example of succeeding by taking on high-risk
management challenges and getting more and more responsibility based on my actual performance. Through luck

and hard work, I ended up getting more and more responsibility until I eventually became Chairman and President of Infonet.

I was also always very close to the nuts-and-bolts operations of the company—close to the actual P & L (profit and loss). I was not political and never have been. I have never been a political person inside the company. I never tried to play politics. It's okay to play politics as long as you're on the winning side. But if you should ever be on the losing side, the organization will quickly neutralize you. It's that simple.

> *My rule is to stay focused. Focus on your responsibilities and don't get involved in playing games.*

My son went to work for Xerox, and about a year later he told me he changed his personnel application and put down "Hispanic."

Apparently that caused a ruckus at Xerox. Some of the people were challenging him, "How can you be Hispanic if you don't speak Spanish? Randy Collazo, is that a Hispanic name?"

I was born in Puerto Rico, so he said, "Hey, my father is Puerto Rican. He's a real Hispanic." I said, "Why did you do this?" He said, "Well, because at Xerox if you're Hispanic or if you're a minority, there is an actual network of Hispanics that try to promote Hispanics." And he found out about this and he felt, "Hey, why not?"

> *It may be fine to join the Latino groups in your company, but what's more important is for you to focus on the things that make your company function.*

If you want to be successful, go into something that is directly related to the P&L of your company. At General Motors it would be engineering or product development. In the case of Xerox I said to my son, "You should go into sales."

> *Latinos should get experience on the P&L of the company, either on the revenue side or the cost side, whatever, the core part of the company. Because there if you can perform, you will have an impact on the company and you will be recognized.*

There's a risk involved with that. In most jobs, if you don't perform, you're out. But people in the early stages of their careers should pursue jobs where if they perform, they get rewards. If you fail, okay, that goes with the territory.

Jose A. Collazo is Chairman and President of Infonet, located in El Segundo, California. He was born in Puerto Rico and graduated from Northrop University with a degree in aeronautical engineering. He has an MBA from Pepperdine University and is a graduate of Stanford University's Advanced Management Program. He started his career as a management trainee for Southern California Gas Company, and became President and Chairman of Infonet in 1988.

The first piece of advice I give to fellow Latinos is to go for the hard jobs that have quantifiable objectives so that your results are not subject to anybody's qualification.

Sara Martinez Tucker
National Vice President
AT&T

I have seen many Hispanics and African-Americans and Asians go into staff jobs, away from the front line, away from the mainstream. I sat back and wondered why that happened. And I started looking at some of the senior people at AT&T who were Latinos or African-Americans, and I realized that the new ones generally just started filling in behind them. At AT&T, you don't see a whole lot of Hispanics in managerial positions out on the front line in customer interface jobs yet.

Another flaw I've seen in our employee resource groups, the associations that support the Latinos, or the African-Americans, is having a feeling of entitlement that if you deliver results strongly at one level it automatically entitles you to the next level. We don't often step back to ask, well, what new skills are required at the next level, and how do I acquire them?

Skills in one level don't translate necessarily to the next, and achievement of results at one level doesn't translate immediately to "I ought to be next in line for promotion."

I counsel and mentor a lot of people who come to me and say, "Look at this. I was a top account executive for seventeen years and I've been passed over for a promotion to sales manager." I've asked them, well, what have you ever done to mentor other AEs or show them that you can become managerial potential by the coaching that you give others?

Sara Martinez Tucker is National Vice President for AT&T Global Business Communications Systems in San Francisco. She was born and raised in Laredo, Texas, and earned a journalism degree and an MBA from the University of Texas at Austin. In 1990 she was the first Latina promoted to AT&T's national executive level. She serves on the board of the National Hispanic Scholarship Foundation, the AT&T Foundation, the University of Texas Natural Sciences Advisory Council, and the Bay Area Council.

━━━━━━━━━━━━━━━━━━━━

I had almost no skills in English. To be successful, you've got to lead, and in order to lead, you've got to persuade, and in order to persuade, you have to be articulate. That's a fact of life.

Enrique Falla
Executive Vice President
Chief Financial Officer
Dow Chemical Company

IF you're Hispanic, and you're not as fluent and as eloquent as other people, you're at a real disadvantage in making presentations and writing reports.

Like many immigrants, I had almost no skills in English—just enough to be able to enter the university. I had to spend six months studying English. In business, I entered the 97th percentile in the United States, that means the top 3 percent. That's why I got a scholarship. But in English, I was in the 29th percentile—71 percent of the people had better English skills than I did!

It was a real challenge for me to overcome the difficulties of language. My bosses said, "Boy, you're sharper and smarter than most of us, but I tell you, there is an area here where you have a difficulty. You do have difficulty in articulating and expressing your views as effectively as you should."

> *Your ability to communicate and your effectiveness in conveying ideas and concepts is critical to your success.*

When I first realized my limitations in this area, I took it hard—my ego was hurt. But I decided to do something about it. With the support of the company, I took some communications courses that were directed toward improving my ability to convey and communicate. They paid for it.

It was very, very critical to my success. You've got to be realistic. If you don't have a perfect command of the English language, you won't be a commentator on CBS until you do!

═══════════════════════

The most important area that you have to really work at is communications.

Jorge Diaz
Vice President and Deputy Program Manager
Northrop Grumman B-2 Division

You have to master oral and written communications, including public speaking. They are imperative in any business.

If I had more years ahead of me I would continue to try to improve in any one of those areas, because there's always room for improvement. I'm not picking on Latins—this is true for anybody. People who control the ability to communicate clearly and concisely are the people who have higher opportunities for success.

Jorge H. Diaz is Vice President and Deputy Program Manager of Northrop Grumman Corporation's B-2 Division in Pico Rivera, California. He was born in Zacatecas, Mexico, earned a bachelor's degree in chemical engineering and master's degree in metallurgy, both from Mexico City University, and joined North American Aviation as a senior research engineer. Years later, as vice president of engineering at Rockwell International Space Division, he was assigned to direct the redesign of the Shuttle Orbiter twenty days after the *Challenger* disaster, and supervised the first two flights in 1988. In 1989, as B-2 chief engineer, he oversaw the first flight of the B-2 "Stealth" bomber.

You've got to want to listen passionately.

Antonio Rodriguez
Senior Vice President
Seagram Spirits and Wine Group

I have a hearing impediment. I wear two hearing aids. But the only handicap I can say I ever really felt was from not listening to people sometimes.

That's become one of the key contributors, I think, to my success—being able to listen and understand people. I really struggle with it. And even to this day, with hearing aids or not, certain times at meetings I miss things. But I'm sensitive to it—I call it listening passionately.

You can learn a lot more with your mouth shut.

You should listen more than talk, and when you speak, you should communicate clearly.

When I speak with some Latinos in Spanish I realize they're smarter than they sound when they're speaking in English.

It doesn't matter whether you're a Latino or you're from Mars. You must be able to listen and communicate clearly, decipher the bullshit, identify the issues, and then articulate your response.

Antonio Rodriguez is Senior Vice President, Strategic Planning, for Seagram Spirits and Wine Group in New York City. He is the son of Spanish immigrants, and was born in Caracas, Venezuela. Tony graduated with a bachelor's degree in economics from Princeton University and an MBA from New York University. He started his career at the accounting firm Coopers & Lybrand. Later he worked at Philip Morris, then joined The Seagram Company in 1983 in the financial planning group. At Seagram, he also served as director of finance for Seagram International, vice president of finance and planning for Seagram Europe, and chief financial officer for Worldwide Spirits and Wine.

Performance is the biggest barrier-buster that exists, but it doesn't work every time.

Solomon Trujillo
President and CEO
U S WEST Communications Group

I went through a lot in my early years, when there were almost no Hispanics in my company, other than in the maintenance areas. When I started, there were no more than one or two Hispanics in management, and we were treated differently from the others.

In Wyoming, my first job was commercial forecaster, which meant I went to various cities and forecast how many telephone lines we would need to install, and how many messages would be sent over our lines.

The world was run then by our local managers. They were the ones who could get you motel rooms. I used to have real trouble with some of our managers. If there were other people from our headquarters offices named Smith or Jones, somehow they never had trouble getting rooms in the nicer motels versus where I'd end up.

Sometimes there would be no rooms and I'd end up staying in the worst place in town. Some people literally refused to help me with connections, meetings, and other things.

> *I've never been one to let barriers or people get in my way. As a matter of fact, when I run into resistance my energy level probably doubles or triples in terms of how I think about overcoming it.*

When I was younger, I got very angry at first. Then, I'd spend my time trying to figure out how I could work around the barriers. Today, I get more disappointed in people than angry, but I try to understand where they're coming from.

I don't care if we're into the mid-1990s, there are prejudices and biases and certain forms of discrimination that still exist. Some of that is a function of human nature because we all have our biases. At the same time, there are others who have greater levels of bias that affect people in negative and destructive ways.

My advice is: understand discrimination, recognize it when it occurs, and deal with it. If you can help educate people, then educate them. If you need to go around people, then go around them. And in a few instances, if you need to go over people and it's the right thing to do, then go over them.

I knew early on that I had to be better than everybody else. I am very competitive. I built this mind-set of competition because there were too many instances where, if I simply performed at the same level as someone named Smith or Jones, the likelihood was greater that the other person would get the job.

In my case, success comes from two things: performance and planning. I'm basically on a path that I described to my wife almost twenty years ago.

I was a director-level manager when I was twenty-five, when the average age to achieve that level was probably forty to fifty. At thirty-two, I was the youngest officer in our company's history. Generation X kids growing up today sometimes think that old fogies like me don't understand that times have changed. I've had some discussions with people in their mid- to late twenties who think that barriers don't exist today, that barriers are just a creation of people who went through the 1960s and 1970s.

The fact is, though, if you hire someone who is a Latino or Latina and someone who is not—both with the same education and levels of achievement—after a five-year period you will find differences in their accomplishments, in their salary levels, and in their positions.

Prejudice still exists. People want to believe that times are different. I want to believe that times are different. However, there are still some structural, systemic issues with which we must deal.

They will be addressed as more of us achieve higher levels. People can look at role models, and I don't mean just Latinos or Latinas looking at Latinos or Latinas. It's the white Anglo-Saxon male looking at a Latino or Latina setting up a company and finding that the entrepreneur is a smart, competent, capable, caring, nondiscriminatory kind of person.

The environment hasn't changed yet. There's all the empirical data that says it hasn't changed. Maybe someday performance will be the one thing that really counts.

Solomon Trujillo is the President and Chief Executive Officer of U S WEST Communications Group, which provides local and long-distance telecommunications services to more than 25 million customers in fourteen western and midwestern states. Based in Denver, U S WEST Communications Group is a $9 billion company with more than 51,000 employees. Mr. Trujillo grew up in a Mexican-American family in Wyoming, began working as a part-time musician in his father's band, Sol Trujillo and his Mariachi Brass, and earned bachelor's and MBA degrees from the University of Wyoming. He began his business career with Mountain Bell in Wyoming in 1974, and was promoted to his current post in July 1995. In 1994, he was elected to the Dayton Hudson Corporation's board of directors. He also serves as chairman of the Tomas Rivera Center and as chairman of the board of trustees of the Center for the New West. He also is a member of the corporate board of advisors for the National Council of La Raza and the Board of Visitors for the Center for Politics and Economics at The Claremont (California) Graduate School. He is on the advisory boards of the Latin American Educational Foundation and U S WEST Technologies, and is a member of the board of directors for the U S WEST Foundation.

I usually start speeches by saying, "What you're about to hear is a Spanish accent, not a speech impediment!"

Carlos Tolosa
Senior Vice President
Harrah's Casinos

I was born and raised in Santiago, Chile. I came to the United States to learn English, and wound up staying here.

My advice is to learn English and learn English well.

If you can avoid speaking another language until you dominate English, do so. I tried to do it on purpose, to not associate myself with Spanish-speaking people while I was learning. Total immersion.

> *Some Latinos murder English. That's going to be a real impediment for them to grow in any organization, until they dominate it.*

When I was a desk clerk at a hotel, one time we had an air-conditioner that was leaking pretty bad and I had to block the room off and leave it for maintenance the next day. I left a note to the general manager, "Room 100 should not be rented this night, the roof is licking." Today, twenty years later, when I see him, he'll still say, "The roof is licking."

When I go to a store and want to buy sheets, I don't use the word. I just refuse to use it because I never know whether it's going to come out right or not! I've made so many mistakes like that. I still do.

Another problem that I've had was that a lot of American people thought that Carlos was my last name. They called me Mr. Carlos. So I dropped the Juan altogether. When people ask me, "Why? It's such a pretty name, how come you don't use it?" I say, I only use it in Latin America, because up here people think I've got a brother, Two Carlos and another brother, Three Carlos!

J. Carlos Tolosa is Senior Vice President, Operations for Harrah's Casinos of Memphis, Tennessee. He was born and raised in Santiago, Chile, came to the United States in 1969, and earned a bachelor's degree in business from the University of Southern Mississippi. He began his career as a trainee at Holiday Inn and worked his way up from director of food and beverage and general manager to become vice president. He also served as chief operating officer and senior vice president of operations for Embassy Suites Hotels.

The concept of politics—that there's somebody out there looking out for you—is rarely true.

James Padilla
Executive Director
Jaguar Engineering and Manufacturing
Ford Motor Company

MY experience says that hard work pays off. I found that people who are aggressive and go after things and get results, get noticed and get promoted. It's as simple as that. So don't wait around for somebody to pick you up and put you in the next spot. It's up to you and it's up to the hard work you put in. Wishing won't make it happen. You've got to do it.

James Padilla is Executive Director of Jaguar Engineering and Manufacturing for Ford Motor Company in Dearborn, Michigan. He was born in Detroit, received bachelor's and master's degrees in chemical engineering from the University of Detroit, and joined Ford in 1966 as a quality control test engineer. His Ford career has spanned manufacturing, product development, environmental and safety affairs. In 1978, he served as a White House Fellow. Since returning to Ford, he has held senior design and engineering positions working on vehicles like the Escort/Tracer, the Taurus/Sable, Mustang, Probe, and Festiva. He was appointed Executive Director of Jaguar Engineering and Manufacturing in 1991, and headed up the launch of the new XJ6 Series.

═══════════════════

Once you become a resource within an organization, then a lot of those other things fall off to the side.

> **Dick Gonzales**
> **Group Vice President**
> **The Vons Companies**

IF you look at most organizations, you're going to find that the successful people do work harder than everybody else.

> *Some people say, "If you're a minority, you have to work 150 percent harder because you're already behind." That may be true, but the fact is that successful people do work harder than everybody else anyway.*

People are successful because they have an edge in some way: they worked harder, but they also worked smarter, were better informed, better prepared, and they became a resource. It's kind of like going to a foreign country. You've got to understand the language and the customs and the rituals before you can really become a contributor.

Dick W. Gonzales is Group Vice President, Human Resources for The Vons Companies in Los Angeles. He was born to a Mexican-American family in the southeastern part of Colorado, where his father was a migrant worker.

===

When building your network, it helps to be creative.

> Alvaro Saralegui
> **General Manager**
> *Sports Illustrated*

WHEN I was looking for a job for nine months in the advertising and media business, I put out a newsletter called *The Saralegui Report*.

There was a media industry newsletter called *The Gallagher Report* which everybody used to read. Fortunately, Gallagher has the same number of letters as Saralegui. So I went to an art store, put *The Saralegui Report* in the same typeface, and sent it around to people who interviewed me, because people always tell you "Stay in touch." You're going to take my call? You're too busy for me to stay in touch.

I kept everyone updated through my newsletter. I would add new contacts to the list as a way of staying in touch without taking their time. Since it was an industry knock-off, it had some charm to it, and they actually bothered to read it.

The secretaries were all laughing. They'd post it on their bulletin board. When I interviewed with other companies, I'd include them so my readers/contacts knew I was interviewing at Condé Nast or *Money* magazine.

Every time I interviewed, I would write, "Circulation

grows by one." "Circulation booming, *The Saralegui Report* hits 12." My potential employers could see I was interviewing everywhere and I wouldn't give up. It's important to let them know how badly you want to get into that industry when you are looking for your first job.

They would think, "Well, he definitely wants to get in the industry and he's got some cleverness or I wouldn't be getting this thing, and it's an ingenious way of letting me know what he's up to without taking up my time, which I appreciate." I stayed in touch with a lot of great contacts that way.

I ended up getting a job as assistant to the general manager of the souvenir program for the 1984 Olympics. How did the headline read in the newsletter? "Saralegui hired for Olympics. *Saralegui Report* defunct. I got a job."

Alvaro Saralegui is General Manager of *Sports Illustrated* magazine in New York City. He was born in Cuba, raised in Westchester County, New York, joined ad agency Benton & Bowles as a media department trainee out of Dartmouth College, then served for three years as *Cosmopolitan Latin America*'s advertising director. He moved to *Sports Illustrated* to work on 1984 Olympic projects and has worked there ever since.

≡≡≡≡≡≡≡≡≡≡≡

I learned real quick that if you do good work, people will respect you. You may not change their mind about women or Latinos; however, you can change their mind about you.

Norma Provencio
Partner
Arthur Andersen LLP

ONE of the mistakes that I see a lot of people make is that they develop a very good relationship with the top people at

a company but totally ignore people at the middle management levels.

If you treat people well and they move to another company they will remember you. They may not call you with
an opportunity until five years from now, but they will call
to give you their business if you were good to them. That's
how I've made my career.

I don't mean to sound like a commercial, but I believe
that the best business relationships are personal.

I joined Arthur Andersen in July 1979. I started as a staff
accountant. At that point about 50 percent of our new hires
were women; however, there were no women partners in
the L.A. office.

In the beginning I had a "whatever it takes" attitude that
helped me to achieve many of my goals. I think that as I
moved along it was not just hard work, but also seeking out
opportunities for visibility.

You can't just be the best technical person. In my business, you also have to be able to sell. I must sell my services
to bring in revenue for my firm. To do that, I must successfully try to be on the leading edge of the changing dynamics
in my industry and in my clients' businesses.

> *No matter what you do, you're going to have to sell.
> You're selling every day. Even though you may not be
> selling a product, you will always be selling yourself.*

I was the first female audit partner in Southern California. When I first made partner, quite a lot of people sent me
notes saying, "You've opened the door!" I really didn't feel
that way, because I had naively spent my whole life believ-
ing everybody is alike, and the fact that somebody is male,
female, black, white, Latino, Asian, or whatever has never
mattered to me.

> *I didn't want to be anybody's role model. But I realized quickly that whether you want to do it or not, you've got a responsibility, and that other people have that expectation of you.*

I encountered some difficulties in my career. I spent my first five years with the firm in the oil and gas industry, and I can tell you there is not a more conservative business than the oil and gas industry. I did encounter some resistance to me personally, but people respect good work, and no matter what, if you do good work, they will respect you as a business professional.

I've always had an easy time dealing with people because I'm a real sports fan. Sports is a tremendous ice breaker. One of the ways that I've always been able to develop relationships with my clients quickly is to talk about the things they're interested in. I play golf. I play tennis and have a great knowledge of sports, such as football, basketball and baseball.

If someone isn't comfortable with you and you get them out on the golf course for a few hours and sit in the cart with them and let them learn something about you, you will have won them over by the end of the day. You will have found common ground.

One of the things I've learned is to enjoy every success, no matter how small. You've got to really sit back and enjoy every success, whether it's a ten-thousand-dollar project or a million-dollar project.

I've always been able to make people feel comfortable with me by sharing something about myself. It opens people up to share something about themselves and usually by the end of the day, we have found something in common.

Norma A. Provencio is an audit partner in the Los Angeles office of the Arthur Andersen LLP, the largest professional services firm in the world. She has over sixteen years of experience in assisting for-profit and not-for-profit clients in the health care industry. She is a member of the Hispanic Association of Certified Public Accountants, and received a BS in Accounting from Loyola Marymount University. She grew up in Monterey Park, California.

===========

Early in my career, I went to work for a small start-up company. I've never worked so hard in my life. I learned many good lessons there.

Margarita Dilley
Director of Strategy and Development
INTELSAT

LESSON number one is you really have to hustle. A small company is the only way you can get that flavor. At a large company, things are so compartmentalized that it's difficult to be close to the customer unless you're in sales or marketing.

Don't give up on something after the first try or even the second. If things really matter to you, just continue pursuing them. Having some real political savvy is critical—the ability to "sell" what you're doing. I think Latin Americans have some natural skills in that respect, and that gives us an edge.

Margarita Dilley is Director of Strategy and Corporate Development for the International Telecommunications Satellite Organization (INTELSAT) in Washington, D.C., a commercial consortium of 134 countries that owns and operates a twenty-one-satellite global system providing worldwide telecommunications services. She held positions of increasing responsibility in corporate finance at COMSAT from 1983 to 1992, becoming treasurer in 1987. Earlier she worked in mergers and acquisitions for the J. Henry Schroder Corporation in New York. She was born in Nicaragua, earned a bachelor's degree in chemistry and history at Cornell, a master's degree in chemistry from Columbia University, and an MBA from the Wharton School.

My sports background prepared me very well for business.

Felix Rivera
Vice President
Johnson & Johnson
Consumer Products Company

THE main industry on Puerto Rico, where I was born and grew up, was the petrochemical industry. It offered great jobs, and was growing, so when I went to college my inclination was to go and try to work in that arena. Fortunately, math and chemistry were my favorite subjects.

I went through school on a sports fellowship. I played basketball as a point guard. Point guards are supposed to be a coach on the court, leading your team into doing the right plays, helping the coach, implementing his game plan.

In sports, you have to be thinking and playing all the time. And I think that really helps you in your career when you have to make a lot of quick decisions. You have half a second to make a decision. In business we have a little bit more, I think we have two seconds!

The team effort, learning from the coaches, learning behaviors from your teammates, they all really relate to succeeding in business.

Knowledge alone won't cut it. You'll succeed by building bridges with people and by building relationships.

Felix Rivera is Vice President, Operations for Johnson & Johnson Consumer Products Company in Skillman, New Jersey, the world's largest health care product manufacturer, with over $15 billion in sales. He was born and raised in Puerto Rico, obtained a bachelor's degree in chemical engineering from the University of Puerto Rico, and started his career as a chemical engineer at Sandoz Company. He joined J&J in 1984 and ran several plants in Puerto Rico before becoming the first person from Puerto Rico to be promoted to vice president of operations in the headquarters office.

Sports is a great equalizer—if you're a good athlete, you get accepted regardless of your accent.

Roberto Muller
President and CEO
The Muller Sports Group

URUGUAY is the smallest of the South American countries. It's a great, great place to grow up. I played soccer, and basketball, rugby, and other sports.

I know of no other element that straddles the world. Think about religion. Obviously, we have Catholics, and Islamic, and Jewish, and Protestant. You have ethnic backgrounds and cultures that straddle different parts of the world. But Guatemala and the United States can compete in some sport and they're not a Third World country and a developed nation. They are just two countries playing each other.

And then you could have China play Saudi Arabia. One is a communist country, the other one is an Islamic country, but they'll play for their lives. The passion of the athletes and the fans straddles any country in the world.

Earlier this year I was in China opening a Reebok store, and a few months ago I had the opportunity to meet in Russia with Mr. Yeltsin. And everywhere I go, I find it fascinating that the one thing that is the common language of the world is sports. It's helped me a lot.

Roberto Muller is President and CEO of The Muller Sports Group in New York City, strategic and tactical advisors to the sporting goods industry. Earlier, he served as president and chief marketing officer of Reebok. He was born in Uruguay, graduated from Leeds University in England, and began his career with DuPont Corporation. In 1975 he founded PONY Sports and Leisure and built it into a $250 million business operating in thirty-seven countries. In 1987 he established Phoenix Integrated, Inc., the parent company of Champion Footwear, Ewing basketball shoes, and Sears/Winner brands.

INSIGHT 2

ADVICE

It's easy for Latinos to get the wrong advice: from peers, mentors, even family. We need to separate the good from the bad. Don't always accept conventional wisdom.

My advice is to go after your dreams with gusto and never take no for an answer.

Concepcion Lara
Founder and CEO
Mediapolis

No one in my family had ever, ever gone away to school. Ever. So it just had never occurred to me or my parents. But then one day I went to the high school guidance office and checked out all the colleges. I came home with twenty catalogues and sat there and read and read and read. When I picked up the Stanford catalogue, I said, "This is where I want to go." But my guidance counselor said to me, "You'll never get in. I should know. My son was a 4.0 and he didn't get in, and his girlfriend was a 4.0 and didn't get in."

I was stunned. I stopped working on my application because I figured she was the authority—she was a counselor, after all. Her experience was getting people into colleges.

As fate would have it, there was a visiting teacher in my high school, who was a Latina, and she asked me what schools I was applying to. I said, "Well, I'm applying to this school and that school, and I was going to apply to Stanford, but my guidance counselor told me that I'll never get in."

It turned out that she had gone to Stanford. And she said to me, "You'd better apply!" So I did.

Then the admissions started coming in, and I hadn't heard and I hadn't heard. I used to go by the name of Connie, because that was the American name imposed on me. So Maria, my teacher, called Stanford and asked if Connie Lara had been accepted. They called back and said I had not.

I went out onto the lawn and sat there. I was crushed. A little later Maria ran out and said, "Oh my God, oh my God. They called back and said, Connie Lara hasn't been accepted, but Concepcion Lara has!"

Despite that, my father refused to let me go. He thought there was no reason for me to go to that school when I could go to a local junior college. It was a complete battle. And he finally relented, at the last possible moment.

My life has always been fraught with a lot of obstacles, but I refuse to give up my dreams for a silly little "no." For me the word "no" doesn't exist. I go after my dreams with gusto!

Concepcion Lara is Founder and CEO of Mediapolis, a multimedia entertainment company in Los Angeles. As general manager/senior V.P. of 20th Century Fox she created and managed Fox's TV network in Latin America. She also initiated and developed both HBO Olé, one of the world's first satellite-delivered cable networks spanning an entire continent, and HBO en Español in the United States.

===

You've got to have a lot of self-confidence. You've got to have a lot of faith in yourself even though everybody around you tells you you're crazy!

Conchita Espinosa
Founder and CEO
Fru-Veg Sales, Inc.

My mother's favorite saying was "You've got to have an education." At eighteen, I decided to leave Miami and go to college in Chicago. We weren't financially well off, but my mother tried to bribe me to stay in Miami by promising me a car if I stayed!

I never put a label on myself. The secret is never to think of yourself as a "minority." If you start labeling yourself, that's when you can become negative toward yourself and your abilities: "Oh, they're not going to give me the business because I'm a woman or a Hispanic." Be confident not to accept labels.

Conchita Espinosa is Founder and CEO of Fru-Veg Sales, Inc., a produce importer located at Miami International Airport that specializes in bringing Latin American fruit and vegetable products to U.S. retailers like A&P, Publix, Acme, and Jewels. She was born in Cuba, attended Barat, a Sacred Heart College in Chicago, and earned a master's degree in Public Administration from Barry University in Miami. She began her career as a produce expediter for International Multifoods in Central and South America.

This is a country of great opportunity. Everywhere I go I convince myself more of that. That's the great thing about this country. We came here without any money, and if you have the brains and you're willing to work, it is still the land of opportunity.

Antonio Rodriguez
Senior Vice President
Seagram Spirits and Wine Group

I grew up in Newark, New Jersey, in the Ironbound section, which is an immigrant-oriented neighborhood. I grew up speaking several different languages. My father was a longshoreman who worked hard and spent his whole life savings to get me through Princeton University. But, he reminded me that we needed to make some money. "What are you going to do for a living?" he asked me.

I came back and said, "Well, I'd like to major in economics. That's practical." It's the closest thing Princeton had to a business degree.

This is something I think a lot of immigrants are going to go through with their parents. It's critical to have support from your parents. My father never had any education. He knew some education was good. But he said, "What's an economist? How much does an economist make an hour?"

Ten years later when I got my bonus check as vice president of finance for Seagram Europe, I bought my father a new car and said, "Dad, that's what an economist makes an hour!"

He got the point. He went to work the next day and said to everyone, "Hey, my son the economist!" Both my parents gave me vital support especially when I needed it most.

Coming out of college in 1979 I had two job offers—one from New Jersey Public Service Electric and Gas at $17,000 and another from the accounting firm Coopers & Lybrand at $12,000. I accepted the $12,000 job, which I thought would be a better experience for me *over the long term.*

My father said, "Wait—$17,000 versus $12,000, please explain—where's the payback on this?" I said, let's be a little longer-term-focused here, it'll work out. In the end, he trusted me.

Another issue that comes up in immigrant Latin families more than in Anglo families is, if you're a successful role model, now everybody else has artificial pressure to be like you. I see it with my cousins. I often get frustrated. I say, "I'm not that special."

I attribute this to the fact that in the neighborhood I grew up in, very few of the kids went on to college. Many more have really not moved socially or economically beyond their parents' level.

My cousins look at me and say, oh, I've got to be like you. I try to tell them, forget that garbage. Be yourself. I'll talk to your parents if you want, to help give you the freedom to make the right kind of decisions. You don't need to hit a certain report card number after two years in the job market that compares to my career.

My parents didn't know what was required to succeed in this country.

Adela Cepeda
Founder and President
AC Advisory

THEY hadn't gone through it themselves. So there were some limitations on how much they could advise their children. So I had to seek out new sources of advice.

Adela Cepeda is Founder and President of AC Advisory in Chicago, which markets investments to institutions and provides financial advisory services to municipal and corporate clients. Earlier, she served as managing director of Abacus Financial Group, an investment management firm managing nearly $300 million in assets for institutional and private clients. She was born in Colombia, received a bachelor's degree from Harvard, and spent over a decade as an investment banker with Smith Barney in Chicago.

We come from very conservative families. That can be a great asset, but sometimes it hurts us.

Linda Alvarado
President
Alvarado Construction, Inc.

WE'RE taught to work hard, follow the rules, pay our bills, go to church on Sunday, and never get in debt. When you don't get in debt it can be very hard to build a business. For Hispanics this is not always a cultural thing that we understand. If there's one risk-taking skill that we need to develop it's that it is okay to do that!

Linda Alvarado is President of Alvarado Construction, Inc., a general-contracting firm based in Denver specializing in commercial, industrial, utility, and heavy engineering projects such as the Denver International Airport and the Denver Convention Center. She is also the first Hispanic owner of a major league baseball franchise, the Colorado Rockies, and is a member of the board of directors of two Fortune 500 companies: Pitney Bowes and Cyprus Amax Minerals. She grew up in a Mexican-American family from Albuquerque, New Mexico, attended California's Pomona College, and got her start in the construction industry as a contract administrator.

My mother taught me if you're reactive and wait for the call to action, you're going to be behind the game.

Sara Martinez Tucker
National Vice President
AT&T

I was born in Laredo, Texas, about 150 miles south of San Antonio, on the Texas-Mexican border. I started working when I was a squirt, nine years old, in my parents' grocery store. I was too small to be a stock person so I sat behind the cash register on a stool.

The name of the store was—are you ready for this?—the Come-n-Shop Grocery. It was a family business. I'll never forget my mother pinching me once when I started arguing with a customer. She said, "The customer is always right."

I wanted to help her understand that the guy was wrong. "No, you don't understand," my mother said. "When we have the goods and they have the money, they're right." So, my mother was my first mentor, I would say. She had no hesitation to pinch me!

That's where my professional life started. That's when I got my Social Security card. She knew I was good with numbers, so I sat there behind the cash register and rang up the sales. But once I got older I was doing everything—

stocking the shelves, dusting, getting minnows out of the minnow tank for the fishermen, hunting licenses. It was a family business. I did it all.

One of the things I learned back then is you could either wait until the customer walked in the door and then go into action, or you could be always making sure you were improving things. My mom taught me to constantly set standards and always look for ways to be innovative, to be different, to keep meeting the customers' needs even when the customers aren't there yet.

=====

My dad was my best boss. He led by example.

Rafael Garcia
CEO
Rafael Architects, Inc.

MY parents both were born in Mexico, and my mother first set foot in the United States after she honeymooned with my dad when she was twenty-six. We're talking first generation here!

My mom's entire family is in Mexico. We went down there every summer. There were seven of us kids. They packed us into the station wagon and we'd drive all the way from Kansas City down to Mexico. Late one night we got lost on a road between Monterrey and the middle of nowhere. I was my dad's co-pilot in the front seat, and everybody else was sleeping in the back, crammed in like sardines. We were lost in the middle of Mexico.

Dad drove up to a light he saw coming from a little house. I said, "Dad, you can't go in there, they're sleeping."

He said, "Hey, we need to eat." We hadn't eaten dinner and then had no place to sleep. My dad kind of screwed up, I figured out. He got out and knocked on the door of the little house. A lady turned on the lights and came out with her robe on. After a forty-five-second conversation, she waved us all in. She fed us and offered to put us up for the night. It was unbelievable.

I was an eight-year-old kid. I had my jaw on the floor in the front seat of the car with the doors locked, thinking my dad could get killed or something! I don't know what my dad said to the lady. He probably just told her the truth.

> *The strongest governing rule about dealing with people in this world is to open your heart up and keep yourself very real and true.*

My dad was an entrepreneur all his life. We had two restaurants, and he was a jeweler, self-made, as my grandfather was. My dad just kind of did things his way. I don't think he ever made over $15,000 a year for a family of nine, but we had food on the table, we looked good, our hair was combed. I started seeing the value system there. And if *he* could do it, shoot, *I* can do it.

He had a jewelry store. We were federally funded, SBA-loaned, in the basement of the Federal Building. Many times, it was just dad and I; sometimes Mom would come down and help put bracelets together. Well, one day a large, very scary man came in. He said, "I brought this watch to you, and you ruined it! Now it won't work!" I thought he was going to hit Dad. I hid behind the wall. I swear, I really thought he was going to hit him. I never saw a man that angry. If that counter wasn't between them, he would have grabbed my dad by the throat.

In the course of five minutes, my dad took this guy's watch, fixed it and gave it back to him. The guy said, "Oh, I guess you're going to charge me now." My dad says, "No, I'm not going to charge you anything."

Suddenly this guy was shaking my dad's hand, smiling and apologizing. In five minutes I saw my dad turn that guy around. I thought, "Man, how did Dad do this?"

He did it by listening to what somebody was trying to say. And by not trying to "own" that person's emotions, but by being sympathetic toward him. If a person felt a certain way, my dad respected it.

My dad took pride in his product, in his work and what he did. He cared about it and he cared about his customers. He fixed the problem and said, "There's no charge for that. I put in a new mainspring. I apologize for that problem." He didn't say, "I screwed up." But he did say, "I apologize for the problem you had with this."

That guy felt shame for how disrespectfully he treated my father. He realized, "You're not like everyone else." And he turned out to be one of our best customers.

My dad's the kind of guy who would walk into an elevator and say to a total stranger, "Wow, red really looks good on you." He had a way of expressing his feelings because he had a love of people.

That really taught me a whole lot about how to deal with people.

Rafael I. Garcia is CEO of Rafael Architects, Inc., a leading architectural firm in Kansas City, Missouri. He earned a bachelor's degree in environmental design, a BS in architectural engineering, and a master's in architecture at the University of Kansas. He began his career as an intern at the age of nineteen and started his own firm in 1987. He has also served as an instructor in architecture at the University of Kansas and El Centro College, and is president of the Kansas City Hispanic Chamber of Commerce. He serves on several key civic, community, and institutional boards, committing his time and love back to the city.

===

It's easy for Latinos to get the wrong advice.

Mario Baeza
President
Wasserstein Perella International;
Chief Executive,
Latin American Operations
Wasserstein Perella & Company

I knew this very talented woman who was Hispanic. She was about to take the bar exam, but the fools she worked with—her colleagues and peers and even some of the partners—said, "Don't worry, don't bother. Nobody studies for it. If you did well in law school, it's a piece of cake."

I kept asking her, "Don't you need to take some time off to really do this?" She said, "No." And sure enough she failed.

She flunked the second time, too. She was shocked. Then all of a sudden, the whole law firm turned against her.

She no longer got responsibility for the big projects. And within seven, eight months she was out of there.

Bad advice is everywhere. And my friend went for the wrong advice, which is very easy to do. I don't even know if the people were being malicious about it or not.

I remember when I was a junior associate and I started working on things called note agreements, which are financial loan documents. These are very complex, tough documents to understand because there are a lot of defining terms: "adjusted consolidated net tangible assets, funded debt." When you first read them, they're like gobbledygook.

I was working on these documents because I wanted to do finance. I took a look at them and I asked, "Does anybody have a book that explains this whole thing?" Everyone said, "No, no, it doesn't exist, doesn't exist." I asked every partner, all the associates, "Is there a book? How the hell do you figure this out?" But everybody said, "Trial and error. You've got to learn by doing it."

> *Be smart enough to know that "trial and error" doesn't work.*

So one weekend I was at the office rereading my corporate finance book from law school, and I discovered a footnote in one of the cases in the text that said: "See Model

Debenture Indenture Provisions, Study of the American Bar Foundation 1967." I went to the library and found the book. It was the holy grail! A classic—sample covenants, agreements, definitions, explanations, everything.

So I took the book home. Over the course of the next month, I reduced all those definitions to index cards and memorized them. Then I studied all the samples and went back to the firm and retrieved from the file room all the note agreements that had been done over the last year. I had a paralegal come and we sat there and copied them, cut them all up and indexed them so I could get my hands on different provisions quickly.

It got to the point that by the time I was only a nine-months associate, fifth-year associates would come to me and say, "Mario, have you ever seen a provision like this?" And I'd say, "Yeah. Let me get back to you on it." I'd close my office door, look at my file and then go back to them in no time and say, "By the way, there's a Connecticut General deal, Petrofina, that was done probably about a year or two ago with the same provision." Bang.

> *Whenever someone tells you you can learn from "trial and error," don't believe it. It's the same version of the same damned story that gets us nine out of ten times. Do the extra homework. Be prepared and do it right the first time.*

> *First and most important, you have to pick the right place to work. It has to be a place that plays to your strengths and minimizes your weaknesses. And to do that you've got to first start with a very critical assessment of just what your strengths and your weaknesses are. It's not just asking what you would like to do or want to do, but what you are naturally good at, what comes easy and in what environments you are most likely to flourish.*

Instead of going out partying, you should be reading and double-reading all the manuals you can find—read, read, read, understand, understand, understand. Talk to as many people as you can. I used to get an assignment and before I sent the draft back I'd talk to five, seven different people about it. Somebody would always give me little insights: "Yeah, but make sure about this twist . . . "

People say, "Give me a quick draft." There is no such animal. It's a total misnomer. There are no preliminary drafts. Make it excellent and flawless the first time.

> *Do a job that's excellent, flawless, without mistakes, no typos. And then you write on it "preliminary draft."*

The worst thing you can do is type up a quick draft with errors and hand it in and get crucified. Then you say, "But, but, but it's preliminary." You're dead.

When you're doing low-level work, it's awfully hard to distinguish yourself. You distinguish yourself by putting in incredible hours, by being dedicated, by paying attention to detail. Believe it or not, I took a lesson from the Xerox guy and learned how to fix the machine. So when I'm down there at one in the morning, trying to copy some documents for a meeting at eight o'clock in the morning and the machine breaks down, I can take it apart, fix the machine and I have my copies. The point is that at 8:00 A.M. I was ready—not with excuses about how the machine didn't work but with my documents and a draft agenda.

When they tell you to take your time, forget it. That's when you should be doing double-time! When they tell you it's trial and error, watch out! If you're a minority, trial and error means you bang your head up against the wall, you make mistakes, you embarrass yourself in public, and the people you're working with may be thinking, "I'm not sure just how bright this guy is." That's what happens, that's the real world. So we can't take our time, we can't do it by trial and error, because when we make mistakes and look like dummies, it sticks for us.

Mario Baeza is President of Wasserstein Perella International Limited and Chief Executive of Latin American Operations for Wasserstein Perella & Company, an investment and merchant banking firm headquartered in New York City with offices in London, Paris, Frankfurt, Tokyo, and Osaka. He was born in New Jersey to a Cuban-American family, and after spending his early childhood in Cuba, returned to the United States and later earned a bachelor's degree at Cornell (in three years) and a law degree from Harvard University. From 1974 to 1994 he was an associate and partner at the New York law firm of Debevoise & Plimpton, becoming the first black or Hispanic man to start as an associate and rise through the ranks to partnership in a major New York law firm. After becoming partner at age thirty he quickly rose to become one of the top billing partners of the firm and a member of its Management Committee. In mid-1994 he was appointed to his current posts at Wasserstein Perella. He has also been a visiting professor of law at Stanford University and a lecturer in law at Harvard Law School. He is a member of the Hispanic National Bar Association, the Cuban-American Bar Association and was the recipient of the Vista 2000 Scholarship Fund Business Award for 1995, granted by the National Society of Hispanic MBAs.

Even if you're paranoid, they can still be out to get you! I'm not really saying they're out to get you, but Latinos are scrutinized twice as hard as other people.

> Christy Haubegger
> **Publisher**
> *Latina Magazine*

I would tell anybody considering working anywhere, if you're a Latino you're probably the only one there, and you're going to be looked at carefully. Stay that extra hour, look over your stuff one more time, because your mistakes are so much worse than anybody else's. I can't underscore that strongly enough.

It's one thing to get into the right company. It's even more of a challenge to get into the right area within a company.

> David Morales
> **President**
> **Latin America**
> **Scientific Atlanta**

A job can sound real sexy, either from the job description or from the guy who's trying to hire you. But once you've got the job, you have to figure out where the real power bases are.

Some divisions are more powerful than others, some individuals within a division are more powerful than others. Who you align yourself with in an organization has a lot to do with your potential success.

When you join an organization you have to find out all you can about the people you're working for. I joined probably the best group in Scientific Atlanta at that time, strictly because of the power base. All the key decision makers were in that group. There were other guys who joined other groups, and didn't do as well.

Unless you're really good at asking a bunch of tough questions in a politically correct way, or have friends within the organization, it's hard to find out where the power bases are when you're not in the organization yet. So what you have to do is, once you're in there, in your first six months, you have to figure out who does what, who's got power, and where decisions are made.

There are a lot of people who work very hard. There are a lot of smart people. But teaming up with the right people in an organization is probably just as important, if not more important, than hard work and sheer intelligence. It really depends on the company's culture and values in determining what's important.

It always pays to find out who the successful people are and somehow get associated with them or join that organization or department.

David Morales is President, Latin America & Caribbean for Scientific Atlanta, a Fortune 500 company based in Atlanta, Georgia. He was born in New York City's Bedford-Stuyvesant neighborhood to a Puerto Rican family. He received a bachelor's degree in economics from Brown University and joined IBM in 1983 as a trainee for its elite sales force. After rising within the IBM sales organization, he left IBM to earn his MBA from the Harvard Business School. He then joined Scientific Atlanta as a marketing specialist, rose to become managing director of Latin America in 1993, then created a $40 million Scientific Atlanta joint venture company focused on distributing cable and satellite products and services to Latin America. Mr. Morales was President and CEO of this company until it was purchased 100% by the other joint venture partner.

=========

OFF THE RECORD
For Latinos, the concept of traditional mentors is often irrelevant. Develop "strategic allies" instead.

37-year-old senior marketing executive in a financial services company

THE old definition of a mentor—somebody in a corner office who takes a "shine" to you because you remind him of him when he was young—is pretty much a thing of the past. It doesn't happen all that often anymore. People are too busy, people are moving too fast. Especially for anyone who isn't automatically seen as part of the power structure in a corporate culture (and Latinos in Anglo-dominated companies usually aren't), I believe it's twice as important to actively seek out and create several "strategic allies" in the company instead.

> *Strategic allies are people in the company you identify as being especially smart and successful. But instead of asking them straight away for advice, try to get to work with them on a project, or a task force, where you can prove to them by your performance that giving you advice a little later will be in their direct strategic interest.*

All the management books keep telling you that having a senior management mentor is critical to your long-term success in a company. This advice is based on the fraudulent assumption that someone like that is automatically going to voluntarily and altruistically "coach" someone whom they may have nothing in common with—ethnically, religiously, etc.

It's up to you to create your own strategic allies. Don't worry if you don't fit their "mentoree" profile. Neither I nor much of America's increasingly diverse workforce does either.

In my case, I joined a large financial services company. While there were hardly any blacks or Latinos in management, I was able to create a strategic alliance with a first-generation Greek-American who was invaluable to me early in my career.

You should also create strategic alliances with other Latinos, of course. They can be an incredibly positive asset for you. However, just because you're both Latinos, don't automatically assume you can lay claim to such a relationship with them.

One of the worst bosses I ever had was another Latino. It wasn't that he wasn't bright. It was that he worried too much about the threat I represented. I had credentials from the country's top schools, I knew the business inside out, was considered a fast-tracker at the company. I looked at this guy as a great opportunity to learn from one of the few Latinos I had ever met in a senior management position.

I was very wrong, and by the time I woke up to the reality, it was too late.

I'd rather have a tormentor than a mentor.

Sara Martinez Tucker
National Vice President
AT&T

I'VE had mentors who come in two shapes. The first group offers me long-range advice and we talk about what I want out of life. The second group are experts on the work I'm doing who help me do my day-to-day job better. Having both is important.

I've also had lots of people who have stroked me and said nice things to me, but when push came to shove they weren't willing to put their name on the line to say, "I support her for that promotion."

It's amazing how many people's spines get jellified all of a sudden.

I learned that the strokers don't necessarily pull you up.

I always figured that if people were willing to take the time to praise you, they'd be willing to put their name on the line for you. It was a surprise to me to learn that some people made others feel good, but it was more of a reflection of their need to hear the same things back to make themselves feel good.

When you look for mentors, make sure you look for people you can learn from who are secure and self-confident, because there are a lot of people who can make you feel good about yourself, but if they have to pull you up in the organization, or if they have to give you hard feedback, they'll shy away from it.

> *A lot of people don't want to give you bad news. I'd rather have someone be hard on me and help me see myself the way others see me, than have someone stroke me and make me feel good.*

One of my bosses pulled me aside and said,"You do very well with people who are like you, who are quick thinkers and who have a lot of energy, but you are really ticking off the people who have been here for twenty, thirty years who don't like the boat rocked. You're going to have to find a way to engage them, because you're going to die in your career if you only engage people like you." Somebody else told me my behavior in meetings was putting people off—that I needed to listen more, talk less. You really need that kind of honest feedback.

Also, don't rely only on Hispanic mentors. I get a lot of

calls from people for advice and the only reason they're call-ing me is because for a time I was the only female or Latino at this level. I keep saying, "There's got to be a lot of other people around you that you can learn from."

When I was in Minneapolis I was the only Martinez in the phone book. In South Texas there were pages and pages of Martinezes. Who do you think I learned from in Minneapo-lis where there was never a Martinez to be found?

So, my first piece of advice for Latinos is to find people you can learn from. My second piece of advice is to avoid the tendency we have to divide Latinos into Puerto Rican, Cuban, and Mexican lines and only support the group where we click. We've got to see the bigger Latino issue and be supportive of any Latino progress in business.

Take help where you can get it!

Christy Haubegger
Publisher
Latina Magazine

THERE aren't too many Latinas who have launched new magazines. This is not a big group. We could all fit together in one stall of a restroom if we wanted to meet!

I find myself making an amalgamation of role models. I take a little bit from here and a little bit from there. They're not all Latinos and they're not all women. Some of my most wonderful mentors have been completely unlike me. Anglo men, for example, who, for one reason or another, think that who I am or what I'm doing is interesting and worth-while.

If you sit around and say, "I'm waiting for someone who looks just exactly like me to reach in and give me a hand," you won't get it. It will take you forever.

You have to look for your role models as you go along, wherever you can find them.

Mentors can't be forced on people.

Natica del Valle von Althann
Managing Director
Citibank

Mentors grow out of a shared experience and mutual respect that develops from that shared experience, and the recognition that the relationship is beneficial to both parties.

Natica del Valle von Althann is Managing Director of Citibank in New York City, the largest banking organization in the United States. She was born in Cuba, raised in Connecticut, and graduated from Bryn Mawr College with a bachelor's degree in political science and Spanish and Latin American studies. She joined Citibank's training program in 1976.

It's important to demonstrate results, to show that you've been able to make things happen, that you've had an impact on your project, your business.

Celeste De Armas
Senior Vice President and General Manager
Nestlé Refrigerated Food Company

ONCE you get that job, you have to actively manage your career. You can't rely on other people to do it.

I have made some mistakes in my career, and one of the biggest ones was when I got so wrapped up in the businesses I was running that I took my eye off the ball and ended up in a job far longer than I should have. I should have been pushing to get cross-functional experience sooner. I should have been pushing to get moved to another division. I lost sight of that. It was a mistake, but I've recovered from it.

> *Active career management is absolutely essential.*

You have to manage your own career. You can rely on the advice from peers, from superiors, and maybe from people in human resources. But you have to manage your career the same way you would manage any other project. And you've got to set goals and timetables and milestones for yourself.

Most companies today are so lean that there's no buffer. Whatever it is you're doing, it's got to have an impact on the business. And the results better be good.

I've never thought that I needed to trumpet what I've done. But I've never been bashful about getting things done and making sure that I had strong points of view. I've wanted to tackle assignments and have hungrily gone after them. But I've never really had a strategic plan for making sure that people knew what I had done.

I can tell you that I've actively managed my career. I've focused a lot of energy on making sure that whatever I did, I did really well. And I made a difference.

You have to be yourself. We all have cultural differences. You don't have to emphasize them. You just have to be yourself without making people uncomfortable about the differences.

Sergio Leiseca
Partner
Baker & McKenzie

IT'S difficult to generalize, but I think that Latinos tend to feel we should develop a business network based on strong personal friendships. You can't always rely on that in business.

Business respect and cordiality don't necessarily translate into personal friendship. We'll deal with each other in business, we'll deal with each other as professionals. That doesn't necessarily mean that there's more to it. It's just that we happen to be respectful of each other in the context of this specific transaction.

It's better to build a network, to use the expression, based upon happy professional recollections that a client might have about your involvement in a transaction, as opposed to the client thinking of you necessarily as a friend. What people look for is expertise and judgment. If you happen to be a friend, that's fine too, but if you're not, that won't disqualify you for anything.

And I don't think people should necessarily expect any favors for being Latino. By the same token, I certainly wouldn't expect people to put up with any nonsense simply because they're Latinos.

Just be yourself!

Sergio A. Leiseca is Partner of the Baker & McKenzie law firm in Miami. He was born in Cuba, moved to Miami as a boy, grew up in New Orleans, and received his bachelor's and law degrees from Tulane University.

Don't become a prisoner of conventional wisdom.

Linda Alvarado
President
Alvarado Construction, Inc.

I don't believe in conventional wisdom. I think conventional wisdom had no role in developing my business, nor historically in any new invention, technology, or new product that's ever come down the line.

Conventional wisdom told me you shouldn't be a boss, because nobody in my family had ever been a boss. We worked for people called "bosses," who didn't pay us right, who didn't treat us right, who had no respect for the Hispanic community. Conventional wisdom in my family said you don't get in debt. Well, sometimes you need debt to achieve your goals.

People who succeed are not necessarily smarter or more persistent, or maybe not necessarily even harder workers. They are people who have the ability to see niches and windows of opportunity.

The Colorado Convention Center was a project that had been on the books for decades in Denver. The land had already been designated. They already knew where it was going to go. Then the city went into recession and the project was delayed. Real estate values went down. One day I sat down for coffee with another contractor. We looked at the project and said, "There's something terribly wrong here. The economics don't work in that location."

We put together a plan that worked, moving the center to a new location. We wrote proposals, we did feasibility studies, we did the work to ensure that the reality would follow our gut instincts. It was a $100 million project. And it was built on time and on budget based on nothing other than four people sitting around a cup of coffee saying, "Maybe those other guys are wrong."

Conventional wisdom said there never would be a major league baseball team in the Rocky Mountains. We don't have big population centers like Los Angeles, Dallas, New York, Chicago, Atlanta. For decades that part of the world had been passed over because the conventional wisdom said that Denver is an old hick town, a bunch of cowboys and cowgirls. It's not a baseball city.

Conventional wisdom also said that Hispanics didn't own major league baseball teams, even though there have been many Latino players. In our first year, the Colorado Rockies broke every attendance record that was ever set, day game, night game, opening day—we set it. And a Latina was one of the owners.

Conventional wisdom was totally wrong!

Don't ever become a member of the "walking dead society."

Andy Plata
Founder and CEO
COPI- Computer Output Printing Inc.

EARLY in my career I worked for nine years at Exxon in the computer area. I was just amazed at how people could go through their day and not have any kind of excitement or care what they were doing. They were just there. I used to call them the "walking dead."

The average tenure for an Exxon employee in my area was twenty-five to thirty years. To work for Exxon back then in a professional area, you had to be in the top of the top of the class. These were extremely intelligent people who were just wasting their time, and losing all of their dreams.

Exxon has changed, but back then getting anything done was extremely bureaucratic. There was no such thing as change.

After working there for a few years, I'd gotten out of the computer room and had a position as a consultant to some of the geologists. There were four or five of us who did this and they gave us a little office that had been a storage room. It was all battered in and the walls were a dirty white.

For two years we asked on a regular basis to have our office painted. It never happened. I had a very nice boss who was one of my mentors, but at the time, he was just trying to do his job as a local Exxon manager. I would ask him and I would hear nothing.

One day after two years, there were painters down the hall and I thought they'd finally sent them to do our office. So I went to my boss and asked him, but he said, "No, they're down there because somebody got a promotion," and at Exxon whenever anybody got a promotion they got a little bigger office. So I said, "Well, just tell them to come down and paint our four walls. It wouldn't take them thirty minutes." "We can't do that," he said. "We have to put in a requisition."

So I informed him that it was now nine in the morning and since I'd been waiting for two years, if we didn't get our office painted by the end of the day, I was going to paint it myself. He kind of chuckled nervously. At lunch I went out to Sears and bought a couple of cans of baby poop yellow paint. I also bought some paint rollers and trays and put them in my office. My boss saw the paint and I told him I was serious about painting my office if he didn't get it painted today.

Sure enough, five o'clock came, the painters left and they had not painted my office. So I stayed after work, changed my clothes and started painting my office baby poop yellow. About seven o'clock, the janitor came in and asked, "What are you doing?" I said, "I'm painting my office. I'm tired of waiting for these bureaucrats." He said, "Let me help!" So we painted together and the results were astonishing.

The next day when my boss poked his head in my office he was speechless. He just turned around and left. We didn't see him until three days later when I was called into his office. Everybody thought I was going to be fired.

"Andy," he said, "I think you made a bad mistake. At Exxon, you can't have a painted office, nobody can. If we let this happen, then everybody will want different colors and it just won't work. So I'm going to have to have these people come in next week and paint your office white again. I understand you're going to be upset, but this is required."

I said, "Do you mean that after two years of asking to have my office painted white produced no results, I paint it baby poop yellow in protest and now you're telling me I am being punished by having my office painted white?"

That's what happened. They came in a week later and painted my office white.

But in that week people who were senior scientists in a building across the parking lot would come just to see the painted office. These were forty-five-, fifty-year-old Ph.D.'s who never came out in the daytime. They'd walk in the office, take a look and say, "A painted wall. How did that happen?"

After nine years and seven months I quit. I was told it was crazy not to wait just five more months to be vested in the retirement plan. But I feared that in five more months, I might have become one of the walking dead, so I quit.

I see people in the walking dead society today who own their own businesses. If you don't have a dream or a goal, you're in the walking dead society as well. It's not just people who work for big companies and it's not just Anglos. Latinos can get trapped in dead-end jobs when they give up their dreams.

The walking dead are extremely contagious. If you hang around them long enough, you'll learn from them. And the only thing they can teach you is how not to have a dream.

Andy Plata is Founder and CEO of COPI- Computer Output Printing Inc., a high-volume computing and laser printing company based in Houston. He grew up in a Mexican-American family in San Antonio, Texas, and began his career as a trainee at Exxon in Houston.

It comes down to the bottom line. You have to compete, you have to be prepared, and you have to deliver.

Phil Roman
Founder, Chairman, and CEO
Film Roman, Inc.

I was born in Fresno, California, in 1930. The Depression just hit in 1929, so things were very, very rough all over. My parents came from Mexico. My first recollection of work was going to the vineyards and picking grapes in the hot summer in Fresno. My mom was a strong influence: "You guys are going to get ahead!"

I got to see *Bambi* when I was twelve years old. And I knew then that I wanted to be an animator. I started drawing. I had a comic strip in the high school paper. I wanted to go to art school, but I couldn't afford it. So after I graduated, I worked in Fresno at the Warner's movie theater. In 1949 I came to L.A. The manager of the theater in Fresno wrote a letter of recommendation to a manager here in L.A. I had $60 in my pocket, I still wanted to go to art school, so I just got on a Greyhound bus and came on down.

Working in the theater, I watched all the Warner cartoons: Bugs Bunny, Porky Pig, Daffy Duck. I got to know all the names of the guys on the screen who created these cartoons. Little did I realize that later on I would be working alongside of them and they would become very good friends of mine.

I went to work for Disney in 1955. It was right before Disneyland opened, and Disney was expanding. They had the *Sleeping Beauty* feature, *The Mickey Mouse Club, The Wonderful World of Disney*. They had commercials, they had shorts, Donald Duck shorts. They were growing and growing.

The experience at Disney was wonderful. It was like being on a college campus, because a lot of young kids were there at the time. There was a lot of energy, a lot of activity. They were shooting live action movies in the back lot, *Davy Crockett* and *Zorro* and things like that. So, at lunchtime you could go back there and walk through the sets. Sometimes they'd be shooting. I thought I was really in Hollywood, and I thought life isn't getting any better than this.

Except that I quit.

I wanted to animate, but I was only an assistant and Disney was so big that there were too many people ahead of me. I knew it would take about eight to ten years to get to where I wanted to be.

I was offered a job in San Francisco to work in a small commercial production house at $150 a week—I was making $95 by the time I quit Disney. So I quit because I felt the opportunities were a little bit better there.

Everybody at Disney told me I was making a dumb move. "This is the best studio in the world. You're going to work at some little studio in San Francisco?" When I came back to L.A., all those people had been laid off from Disney in a big cutback. All the people who told me I made a dumb move leaving Disney wound up getting laid off!

The animation business has been very, very open to Hispanics, going way back to the 1930s and the early days of animation. At Disney there were a lot of Mexican-American guys, like Rudy Zamora, Tony Rivera, Manny Perez, Bill Melendez. The list goes on and on.

> *There have been some great contributions made to the animation business by the Hispanic community, because we're very creative and have a lot of imagination.*

The great thing about this business is that you're judged only on what you do, not who you are. And all of this other stuff is totally immaterial. It's just "How good is that person's work?" Did he deliver, did he contribute? That's all. You walk through my studio, you see all kinds of people. All kinds of ages. Only what gets on the screen is important.

> *I try to think that being Mexican-American hasn't been a factor in my success, positive or negative. I don't know what people think—but the way I feel is if somebody doesn't like Mexicans it's not my problem, it's his problem. And if I start getting involved with that person, all of a sudden it's my problem.*

I have other things I want to do. I'm not going to solve his problem. It just takes up too much energy. And you can be expending that energy in real, very positive ways, rather than starting on little ridiculous things that get you nowhere.

Your product should speak for you, nothing else. Absolutely. That's the only way you can be judged. Otherwise you're not going to make it.

Phil Roman is Founder, Chairman, and CEO of Film Roman, Inc. in North Hollywood, California, one of the country's top TV and movie animation companies and animator of *The Simpsons*. Born in Fresno, California, he attended the Los Angeles Art Center and served four years in the air force. He was an animation designer, artist, and director from the 1960s through the early 1980s, for companies like Disney, Chuck Jones, MGM, and Warner Brothers, on classic movies and TV shows, including *The Incredible Mr. Limpet*, *The Grinch That Stole Christmas*, *Garfield*, *Tom & Jerry: The Movie*, *The Critic*, *Bobby's World*, and *The Simpsons*. Since he founded the firm in 1985, revenues have increased from $300,000 to $35 million.

No matter what happens, the show must go on.

Marcos Avila
President
Cristina Saralegui Enterprises

THE worst day of my recent history was the day I lost my last client. I felt really, really terrible. I came to tears. I saw defeat right in my face. My best day was five minutes later, when I decided to go ahead and not give up. I decided to stick it out, and a week later I had a new client and things took off after that.

When you start a business, sometimes you tend to overextend yourself. You're opening a business from nothing, especially a service-oriented business. You may tend to hire too many people or you tend to get a super-big office, but remember: the only thing your clients really care about is results.

Before I started my own company, I really only had one boss—Emilio Estefan. He's an extremely successful producer. He's done very, very well with his wife, Gloria, and Jon Secada and others. The thing I learned from him is that the show has to go on, no matter what. You have to be good to your people, but no matter what happens, the show will go on with them or without them, because business must be taken care of.

Sometimes people fall asleep on their successes, which is a ticket to disaster. My business, television and entertainment, is very fast-paced. You're only as good as your last hit. The competition is tremendous. Television is like a monster that needs continuous attention and continuous promotion. There are a lot of families that get fed from what our company does. If you're not doing your share, you're going to be replaced. It doesn't matter who you are. If I don't do my job, I'm going to have to be replaced. The show must go on.

It's very important to work very hard, but more important to work very smart. And don't give up. If you think you can accomplish it, don't give up. Go for it, go for it, go for it.

Marcos Avila is President of Cristina Saralegui Enterprises, a multimedia company headquartered in Miami Beach, that co-produces *The Cristina Show*, one of the top-rated programs on the Univision television network, and is distributed to eighteen countries throughout the Spanish-speaking world; *Cristina: La Revista*, one of the highest-circulation Spanish-language magazines in the United States, with major distribution in Latin America; and through radio production subsidiary Magikcity Communications, Inc., packages Spanish-language radio programs including *Cristina Opina* and *Somos Hispanos,* hosted by Ricardo Montalban. He grew up in Florida and began his career working with Gloria and Emilio Estefan as an original member of the Miami Sound Machine. In the 1980s he ran his own entertainment management and public relations company, Magikcity Media.

Persistence. Never give up. No matter how menial your job is, it's an important part of your business. If you do it right and give it your best effort, you're going to succeed.

Roberto Suarez
President, Miami Herald Publishing Company
and Publisher, *El Nuevo Herald*

IN a few short months I went from president of a major financial institution, Financiera Nacional de Cuba, to being unemployed and unable to find a job.

My family left Cuba to come to Miami right before the Bay of Pigs, in April of 1961. I couldn't get a job no matter what. We had nine kids and no money, because there was no way to get money out of Cuba.

My first job was as a housecleaner. It turned out I was allergic to the chemicals in the cleaning fluids, so the first $20 I earned had to go straight to buy medicine. Then a nephew of mine said they're hiring at the *Miami Herald.* I asked him, "What's that?" He said, "I don't know." I said, "Well, let's go check it out."

The *Miami Herald* needed people to work in the mail room. In the newspaper business the mail room isn't where you send out mail. It's where you package the newspapers. They come out of the press, you ship them to the loading dock, and they're loaded into trucks. I spent the whole night packing and loading papers. When the shift was over, they told me to come back the next morning. I went home and my wife tied towels with ice on my forearms because they were all swollen. That was my second job.

The first paycheck I got from the newspaper went straight to buy milk for the children. The Cuban Refugee Center gave you powdered milk, powdered eggs, rice, and some strange-looking meats. The kids were drinking a lot of powdered milk, and they were really skinny, so we went and bought real milk for the first time. That was a good experience.

While I was in the mail room, I took aptitude tests and they told me I would never make it any higher in the production area because I didn't have any mechanical abilities. After a little while they learned I could do other things, and they had me do the payroll for the department. Then they asked me if I wanted to be a supervisor, my first opportunity to advance a little bit.

I went to the personnel director and said I thought I could be more valuable on the business side than working in the mail room. He told me I should be very happy because I had done in a year or two what it takes thirty years for other people to do—and I didn't know anything about the newspaper business. I could understand that, but I didn't give up.

Soon after that I heard about an opening in the accounting department, so I went straight to the department manager. He asked me, "What do you know about the newspaper business?" I said, "Not much, but I guarantee you in six months I'll know everything that needs to be known." He laughed.

So he hired me as the accountant for the subsidiary operations of *The Miami Herald,* and I eventually became chief financial officer and learned the business from the bottom up. You've got to have faith—faith in yourself.

Roberto Suarez recently retired as President of the Miami Herald Publishing Company and Publisher of *El Nuevo Herald* in Miami, a Knight-Ridder newspaper. He was born in Havana, Cuba, and gradu-

ated from Villanova University with a BS in economics. He also
served as president and general manager of *The Charlotte Observer.*

━━━━━━━━━━━

My father always taught me that you have to diversify.

Eduardo Paz
Chairman and President
Teleconsult, Inc.

MY father taught me that you should be focused, but never
rely on just one client or product. You should trust people
but always cover your tail. You should always have alternatives and backup plans in case the worst happens.

Eduardo Paz is Chairman and President of Teleconsult, Inc. in Washington, D.C., an international telecommunications consulting company. He was born in Bolivia, raised there and in the Washington,
D.C. area, and earned bachelor's and master's degrees in engineering
from Cornell University and is a Ph.D. candidate at George Washington University. He joined MCI in 1984 to work on transmission planning in the firm's fiber optics group and stayed until 1989. He bought
Teleconsult in 1990 and is currently doing business in Central and
South America, Europe, the newly independent states of the former
Soviet Union, Africa, Asia, and the Middle East.

━━━━━━━━━━━

You have to be responsible for your own destiny. You can't rely on some employer to be the person who makes all the decisions.

Jim Saavedra
Senior Vice President
Union Bank

ONE of my most valuable experiences happened in 1977,
when the company I worked for was put up for sale. I had

risen to the position of vice president by then. I started out as a systems analyst. Those of us in senior management positions were given a golden parachute and told that our services were no longer required by the new acquiring organization.

It was a big shock at the time, but it forced me to go back and really rethink my priorities, figure out what was important, set some personal goals and focus on achieving them. It was a wake-up call. And the end result was that I went to work for a highly entrepreneurial company in a completely different industry. I stepped out of the financial services industry and went to work for an airline. And I spent two very valuable years working for an entrepreneur who was very innovative and radical in his thinking.

Don't have any fears of changing employers or changing industries. Consider yourself a skilled commodity. Be clear about what your strengths are and be willing to learn from every single situation.

If you come to the decision that you really can't learn much more in a job, then it's time to leave. It's not a question of whether it's good or bad, it's just the cold reality of the situation. Deal with the reality, don't get hung up on whether it's right or wrong.

C. James Saavedra is Senior Vice President of Union Bank in San Francisco. He was born and raised in Denver, attended Regis University and Naval Officer's Candidate School, and began his career as a management trainee at a thrift company. He also held senior management positions at Western States Bankcard Association, World Airways, First Nationwide Bank, and Wells Fargo Bank.

Leave behind friends, not enemies.

Fred Estrada
Chairman and CEO
Hispanic Publishing Corporation

As a young man when I had to change jobs I always gave my employers as much notice as possible and made sure they fully understood why I was leaving. If you do it properly and in an orderly manner, more often than not you will keep your friends and mentors even though you've left the company. That is why, over the past forty years I've been able to maintain many successful business relationships with former corporate employers and associates.

In business sometimes you do what you have to do, but always do it with professionalism and respect and you won't burn your bridges.

Fred Estrada is Chairman and CEO of Hispanic Publishing Corporation which publishes *VISTA* and *HISPANIC*, the magazines serving the U.S. Latino community with the largest national circulation.

═══════════════

A challenge is one of the most terrific things that can happen in your career. And change is really an opportunity, not a negative. Even if it's a negative in your initial perception, it's up to you to turn it into an opportunity.

Jorge Luis Rodriguez
Chief Marketing Officer
AVANTEL, MCI Communications

I came to MCI in 1979 in an entry-level role in business development, right out of Georgetown. MCI was just getting started then. My brother is about twelve, thirteen years older than I am. I told him, "I'm working for this company called MCI and we're competing against AT&T." Early in his career he had worked at AT&T. He said, "You guys are crazy. You're just going to get killed." Today he'd have a very different view.

I worked in a variety of roles with MCI from 1979 to 1986. The company had a very entrepreneurial, go-getter, upbeat, irreverent atmosphere, where you felt you could really contribute to the success of the business. I learned that there's nothing that you can't do to turn something to your advantage. It's all in your mind-set and attitude. That's something I acquired at MCI—a fledgling little company going up against a giant like AT&T. In that corporate culture, you had to be very resilient. If you believed in something you had to push for it and sell it and be aggressive about it. You couldn't just wait for someone to come and say, okay, well, what do you think?

I left MCI in 1986 and went to a competitor called Sprint. I did it because an individual I had worked for, who was a mentor of mine, offered me a fabulous opportunity to reintroduce Sprint to the market and move it into a new arena of marketing. The famous "pin drop" campaign with Candice Bergen is my baby.

I left MCI because I wasn't having fun anymore. It had become too comfortable, not challenging enough. It wasn't hitting my desire to be entrepreneurial, more aggressive, more in-your-face, more irreverent. That's an environment I thrive in, an environment where you can be risk-oriented. You pay the penalty if you mess up, but you get the reward if you don't. This was the environment that had challenged me so much; an environment I knew MCI could never really lose, and would one day bring me back.

In 1994 I came back to MCI to launch what I call our adventure into Mexico and Latin America. We have a venture that has zero revenue today, but within five years will likely be worth at least $1 billion plus in business. We're building a network from scratch. We don't have, for all practical purposes, a sales force, a billing system, a product, anything. It doesn't exist. It's obviously a very exciting opportunity to build a company from zero. And it's just the kind of challenge I like.

Jorge Luis Rodriguez is Chief Marketing Officer of the AVANTEL venture of MCI Communications Corporation in Washington, D.C. He grew up in Cuba, Spain, and Puerto Rico, and graduated from Georgetown University with a bachelor's degree in finance. He joined MCI in 1979.

═══════════════

You have to be able to sort out good advice from bad advice, even from people like your parents.

Marcela Donadio
Partner
Ernst & Young

YOU have to decide what you want to do, you have to be willing to take advice, but then you also have to be willing to make your own decisions, and then you have to go for it.

Marcela Donadio is a Partner at the Ernst & Young accounting firm in Houston. She was born in Panama, obtained an accounting degree from Louisiana State University, and joined Arthur Young, a predecessor firm of E&Y, in 1976 as a trainee. She became partner in 1989.

═══════════════

"Dime con quien andas y te dire quien eres."

Anthony Xavier Silva
Chairman, Co-founder, and CEO
Corporate Systems Group

THERE was a Spanish poet named Miguel Unamuno who was part of a poetic association called the Generation of 1898. He said *"Dime con quien andas y te dire quien eres,"* which means, "Tell me who you're with and I'll tell you who you are."

Associate with only the most hardworking and genuine, honest people. Establishing these people as mentors will create the right role models for your life and career.

Anthony Xavier Silva is Chairman, Co-founder, and CEO of Corporate Systems Group in Miami, one of Hispanic Business magazine's top 500 Hispanic-owned businesses. He was born and raised in the Miami area and began his career as a computer product salesman for IBM and Nynex. He started Corporate Systems Group in June 1990 with only two people. Today the company has 40 employees, and continues an extremely impressive growth rate, with anticipated 1995 revenues of $10 million. This growth rate should qualify Corporate Systems Group as one of the fastest-growing Hispanic-owned businesses in the United States.

___

Don't let your surname prevent you from getting involved in anything that you want to get involved in.

Jamie Cuadra
President and CEO
Ransom Original Soul Wear

DON'T pigeonhole yourself into any particular area just because of who you are or how your name reads. You've got to be open to everything and get involved with everybody.

Jamie Cuadra was recently Chief Financial Officer of Cal-State Lumber Sales, Inc. in San Ysidro, California, one of *Hispanic Business* magazine's top 500 Hispanic-owned businesses. He was born in Nicaragua and raised in San Diego and San Francisco. He is currently President and CEO of Ransom Original Soul Wear, a contemporary Christian apparel company based in San Ysidro, California.

INSIGHT 3

TREMENDOUS ASSET

In the new global and multicultural economy, your Latino heritage is a tremendous asset— adaptability, sensitivity, language.

For my Latino brothers and sisters, the advice from my experience is move, keep an open mind, don't seek linear careers that go to the top because they don't exist. Seek experiences where you can be enriched, where you can leverage your cultural diversity.

Enrique Guardia
Group Vice President
Kraft General Foods USA

I wanted to leverage my cultural difference into advantages and put them to work. The company I work for, General Foods, had major international operations, so I chased that opportunity. I was advised by everybody that international was sort of a dead-end path—out of sight, out of mind. But it struck me that going to Europe would give me so much cultural variety that I could really put to use.

I was offered an opportunity to go to England and I took it instantly, although the job was at a lower level than the job I already had. Then after being in England for a while, the company said, "The place we need you is in France. But we must tell you that nobody survives France. The French are impossible."

I don't know whether I was dumb, but I thrive on challenges. I knew a little bit of French, and I knew I could be as French as the French are. So I became one of them. I lived among them, not where the expatriates lived. And I learned to master the language, which was a tremendous amount of work.

It was probably the defining experience of my career, because I went in there with very few expectations from anybody that I would cover myself with glory or that I would succeed. In fact, after three years they asked me to take over the whole European R&D group.

> *Being multicultural and multilingual, particularly in today's world, is a huge asset. Chase opportunities and leverage your differences.*

The typical American education makes you very afraid to take that kind of risk. A typical American manager in Paris was there bitching and moaning about how Paris was not like Chicago. For some reason, it's very difficult for Americans to learn other languages, to deal with other cultures. But you become a better competitor by choosing the arena that you compete in. Paris to me was a great example of that. Most Americans just couldn't wait to get out of there. I fell in love with Paris, and I consider myself part Parisian today!

I had very little supervision because my bosses were miles and miles away. So the decisions were mine. About fifteen years and eight promotions later in headquarters, I was supposed to be running the world, and I used to say the difference between Paris and here was that in Paris I didn't have a boss. I was my own boss. In headquarters I've got twenty-three bosses.

I always tell Latinos who seek me out for advice that what will separate them from the pack is to move. Because so few people are willing to. Move for a career, don't move for the next job. Get the experience, get the ability to be your own boss. That is becoming more and more relevant because in a place like my company, which now has people all over the world, there is an incredible inability for people to say, "Yeah, I'll take that job, I'll move." I'm not just talking about Europe or Asia, I'm talking about Chicago. Getting people to move from New York to Chicago is as difficult as getting people to move overseas.

> *Some people tell me cultural diversity is a handicap.*
> *I don't accept that. I don't think it's a handicap at*
> *all. In today's world it is absolutely terrific for peo-*
> *ple to speak Spanish, to have lived in other cultures,*
> *to understand the ways that different people behave.*

Dr. Enrique J. Guardia is Group Vice President of Technology for
Kraft General Foods USA in Tarrytown, New York. He leads all re-
search and engineering for the global consumer goods company. He
was born on Christmas Day in Panama, and earned bachelor's and
Ph.D. degrees from the University of Washington in Seattle. He joined
General Foods as a chemist and rose through positions in Battle
Creek, London, Paris, and Brussels to his current job. He is a trustee
of the National Hispanic Scholarship Fund.

**American business is becoming more and more
global. That makes your ethnicity more and more
of an asset.**

Jose Collazo
Chairman and President
Infonet

I T's probably reverse discrimination. If you're an American
from Ohio, it can be very difficult for you to be accepted internationally. International people can say, "You have no
idea what happens outside of the U.S." They look down on
you.

Hispanics should get experience on the international side
of business if they can, because there your ethnicity is an
asset, either for the language, or for the fact that you're
often more accepted as someone who understands about
different cultures.

If you're going to do business internationally, make sure to retain your Latin roots.

Andres Bande
President
Ameritech International

THE most important thing for a Hispanic is not only to think as an American if you want to compete in international business. You must adopt an international mentality.

A Hispanic has to draw from his Hispanic origins, his Hispanic culture, his Hispanic ancestry and project himself internationally. If people around him don't like it, he only has to say, "Listen, you hired me because you wanted me to bring to you the value of an international, cosmopolitan, multicultural working environment." That's very important.

America is a rich nation because it's cosmopolitan and diverse. Latinos will play an important role in bringing the best of America to international business.

Andres Bande is President of Ameritech International in Chicago, which develops and operates global investments in telephone network privatization, wireless technology, and directory publishing. He earlier served as executive vice president of U S WEST International and has worked for twenty-five years in international telecommunications. He is Chairman of the Chicago Committee on Hispanic Education, and is President of the Hispanic Business Roundtable. A native of Chile, he received his law degree from the University of Chile in Santiago and a master's degree in politics and international law from Oxford University in England. During the Bush administration, Mr. Bande was chairman of the White House Commission on Educational Excellence for Hispanic Americans.

Latinos offer the best of both worlds—the innovativeness and creativity of the Latins, plus the discipline of the American system.

Roberto Muller
President and CEO
The Muller Sports Group

WHEN I went to work for DuPont in South America, I learned how professional the Americans were. Latinos are more flexible, more creative, more innovative, and more adaptable to the global society and can also bring the professionalism and efficiency of traditional American business.

We adapt ourselves to economic changes more easily than Americans or Europeans do. So we're much more flexible in the global society. You see a tremendous amount of international executives now coming out of the Latin ranks.

I like to take the best of the two cultures and integrate them into my own life.

Gerardo Villacres
General Manager
CBS Americas

I came to the United States as a very young man without the language. I had taken some courses in English but it's another thing to be able to speak the language. What's more important is the cultural shock that you receive coming from a very different culture. It took me about five years to feel more comfortable with the American culture, to be "biculturated," so to speak.

I was let go from a job that I had in the aerospace industry. My wife and I made a conscious decision for me to continue to go to school in the daytime because I was changing professions. For those two years my wife supported me. I was collecting unemployment for a while. They were tough times.

The man in the Latin culture is supposed to be supporting the wife. The wife is not supposed to be supporting the man. It's not very well accepted. But I would have to say that even her parents, her family who lived in the United States, everybody was supportive of what we were doing, which was very unique and interesting.

> *We have to be open-minded to different things from other cultures that are positive and good and that can help us overall, and not be close-minded and say, "This is the only thing that's right."*

I don't think it's acculturation as much as biculturation. I think that in order to succeed in this country, you have to biculturate yourself. That's the toughest part for many Latinos, to be able to feel comfortable with the duality of two different cultures.

To me it means feeling comfortable with the language, being able to laugh at the David Letterman jokes and still go shopping for plantains!

Gerardo Villacres is General Manager of CBS Americas in New York City, a radio network providing news, sports, and entertainment to affiliates across the United States and Central and South America. He was born in Riobamba, Ecuador, and raised in Quito, Ecuador, came to the United States at nineteen, and obtained a bachelor's degree in accounting and business from Rutgers University. He was recruited by CBS at Rutgers to join the CBS internal audit department. He also worked in business affairs and music video production for CBS Records.

We've got to stop talking about Latinos as moral obligations, and start selling ourselves as a business asset.

Enrique Guardia
Group Vice President
Kraft General Foods USA

I hear much about the moral obligation and the ethical obligation of hiring Latinos and blacks. And I respect that. But we're in business for business. And in business what you do is sell something to a consumer and the consumer is king. So I say to my Latino brothers and sisters, "Look who we are selling to." We are selling to ethnic populations in the U.S.A. and around the world.

> *Understanding your consumer is the most incredibly important requirement to be successful in business. We cannot survive without understanding blacks, without understanding Latinos. Who better to give us that insight than Mexicans, and Puerto Ricans, and Cubans, and African-Americans?*
>
> *"Diversity" may not be the right word. "Diversity" implies something different from the norm. Well, the norm in much of America today is multicultural consumers.*

I am a Latino, I speak Spanish, I understand how we eat, I understand what my mother cooked. That's a profound asset that we often don't talk about because we get all wrapped up in moral obligations and issues like affirmative action. I'm not knocking them. I'm just saying you should start by thinking not so much about how to overcome a handicap, but about how you can leverage what you are.

We should all be humble enough to talk about our failures and learn from them. One of the things that I think we missed the boat on in General Foods was ethnic marketing and ethnic products very early on. I'm in the food business, so we're always talking about the food people eat. A mistake I made years ago was trying to sell the Latino asset to my company by saying, "This is terrific because this is what Latinos eat." Frankly, it would have been a much better position to say, "Because of the ethnic influence of the Latinos, this will become the food that Anglo-Saxons and blacks and Europeans and Japanese will eat."

If I had to do it again, I would have packaged it differently. I would have said, "The time will come when everybody, including Peoria, Illinois, is going to be eating black beans and rice and hot sauces!" If you go to a regular supermarket today you find everything that I used to eat at home forty years ago. I used to not be able to find anything other than Tabasco in my supermarket. Now there are black beans, Mexican salsas, and Jamaican, and Louisianan.

I should have had the vision to say, "This is a way of the future," as opposed to, "Gee, this is the way my people eat." Positioning and packaging the project you're putting forward are critical. It's much better to sell an idea because it's a good business idea than to talk about moral obligations and ethical imperatives. And that includes selling yourself as an asset.

What is diversity?

Carlos Tolosa
Senior Vice President
Harrah's Casinos

PEOPLE talk about diversity, but not a lot of people understand what it means. They only see it from the view of the color of the people and not necessarily from the culture and the values that can be so different depending on where they came from.

═══════════════════

If you don't grow up in a traditional nuclear family, don't think it's a handicap. On the contrary, I think it can be an asset. It can be an empowering experience.

Angel Martinez
President and CEO
The Rockport Company

MY mother and father divorced a little after I was born. I went to live with my grandmother's sister. Then when I was three years old, she and her husband decided to immigrate to the United States and we moved to New York City. They were my guardians but they were really my parents. They were elderly people. It was like being raised by my grandparents.

My guardians moved from New York City to California in 1967. They loved me like their own son, and I loved them as my parents. By the time I came along, they knew that the important thing in life was to teach kids to be accountable and be responsible for their actions.

I remember having a very long leash as a kid, but I remember always having this tremendous sense of responsibility. I felt a sense of responsibility about more than myself. No one had to tell me to call home at eleven o'clock every night if I wasn't going to be home at eleven. I did it.

A lot of Latinos find themselves being raised by an extended family, like I was. And the family was everything. Because between my guardians and their children and their children's kids, who were about my age, it was always a very tight, very closely knit family.

I always had an entrepreneurial bent, even when I was a kid in the Bronx. I used to mop buildings on Saturdays and Sundays, three dollars a building. When we got to California, I wanted a paper route, so I got a paper route.

When I was fifteen, one of my guardians passed away. My other guardian was also pretty sick, and we had no choice but to go on welfare, Aid for Families with Dependent Children (AFDC). They're now talking about eliminating that program completely, forgetting that there are lots of people who have no choice. This woman was seventy years old, didn't speak English, and had a heart problem. We lived in a little Victorian duplex and we had to get AFDC and food stamps.

I hated that. I hated even being seen using the things. Someone else in my family said, "Well, you know, you have to do that, you're poor." I remember having an emotional outburst at the word "poor."

I didn't feel I was poor, never ever felt I was poor. Not having money had nothing to do with being poor. We didn't have any money. I thought that was a temporary situation. The fact is I never felt poor in any way, shape, or form and I felt very, very rich in terms of who I was and what I was about.

Competitive running helped me get through the next three or four years. I dedicated myself to it and had a lot of success, and by the time I got out of high school it had grounded me in who I was and how I felt about myself, for the rest of my life.

In my family, the only important thing to be was an engineer, or a *médico*. In college I did what I felt was the dutiful thing. I studied premed, and then realized I hated this. I think a lot of people are pressured into going to college so they can be somebody. People neglect to tell them they already are somebody. The purpose of a university isn't to create a job for you. The purpose of a university is to further learning and enhance knowledge.

> *Too much emphasis is placed on getting a paycheck. Not enough emphasis is placed on the process of learning. If you can discipline yourself around the process of learning and gaining knowledge, then just about any door is open to you down the road.*

Angel Martinez is President and CEO of The Rockport Company of Marlboro, Massachusetts, a subsidiary of Reebok. He was born in Cuba, raised in the Bronx, and graduated from the University of California at Davis, where he was an all-American in cross-country and track. He joined the then-fledgling Reebok as West Coast sales representative in 1980, led the company into the explosive aerobics shoe market, and championed the firm's Human Rights Now awards program. He became head of the $300 million Rockport unit in 1994.

I'm a firm believer that you have to be humble, and you have to really want things bad enough to get them. There's no such thing as needing or wanting something and not getting it.

Fernando Mateo
Founder, Chairman, and CEO
Carpet Fashions

BEING one of twenty-five children, as a child things weren't great for me in terms of having access to a lot of money. We had the necessary things in life—clothing, food, good schooling—but I grew up very hungry.

I remember kids on our block always had Converses or Pro Keds. And I always had Skippies. Kids used to laugh and say, "Look at him with the Skippies." So, at a young age

I always had the burning desire to have better things. I always feared rejection. I always feared being less than anyone.

I felt very intimidated in school. The hip kids were all smoking pot, doing coke, and doing all kinds of wrong things. I got into that group. A few months later I realized, "What the hell am I doing with these people?"

I found a part-time job to keep me busy after school, working for a Jewish family selling baby furniture. I was a stock boy. I used to hide behind the boxes to hear the owner of the store selling. He was the most brilliant salesman I have ever heard, because he was hungry.

> *When you're hungry, when you're determined, you can make anything happen. The necessity of needing something drives you to figure out what you have to do to get it.*

But when Spanish customers walked into the store, he couldn't sell to them because he didn't speak Spanish. So I started selling to them. The same things he used to say I used to say, but in Spanish. I knew every product from its nuts to its bolts. I knew every crib, every stroller, every swing set, everything. I could take them apart and put them back together. I knew the safety regulations. I understood that you needed to know your product in order to sell it.

Pretty soon, I was selling $5,000, $6,000 to people who would come in to buy a stroller. I'd sell them a crib and a bassinet and a chest, and a hutch. I felt that if I gave them a reason to believe in me, if I gained their trust, I could do anything. So I gained their trust with an item by educating them about it, showing them why this was better than this, this, and that. And I started to just sell, and sell, and sell.

At fifteen I dropped out of school because I wanted to make money, and I learned a skill. I learned how to install floors because my brothers all were in the floor-covering business. At seventeen I got married and started my own business, Carpet Fashions. I'd get up at four o'clock in the morning and throw cards under doors. They'd call the store and say, hey, you put a card under my door, I need some linoleum, I need some carpet, could you give me an estimate? I'd tell them, well, I'm very busy right now, but in the meantime I wasn't doing diddly. I was in an empty store sitting behind a desk, waiting for people to come in.

I left the store one day and thought, "I've got to get credit." I walked into this credit manager's office, and I locked the door behind me and I dropped to my hands and knees and I begged him. I said, "Please give me a line of credit. Give me something. Five hundred, a thousand, anything." He said, "Kid, get off the floor. I'm going to give you a credit line because you're going to make it."

I humbled myself, but I got what I wanted.

If you walk outside here every building is for sale, everything has a price. It's just a matter of who can afford it, and who can't. We live only one time, and life goes by very quickly. I'm thirty-seven now. I can't believe where the hell the years have gone!

I went from being a child to being a man. I never had an in-between. I don't have a high school education. I don't have a college education, though I have honorary degrees from colleges. But I've got common sense and I have the desire to be somebody.

I'm humble. And I'm hungry. And I'm not ashamed to ask.

It's nice to live with luxuries and things, but it's also nice to remember who made you who you are. I've never forgotten where I've come from and who I am. And I always go back into my community and try to do something to better my community. I do things to give a push to my people.

I don't like blaming whites for conditions in the projects we live in. Why blame them? They've never lived here, they've never come here. Don't blame others. I will never say that I'm not successful because of someone else. No, I'm not successful because I decided not to be successful.

There's no such things as bad breaks in life. If you're paralyzed, if you're sick, an ailment, that's one thing. But if you're healthy, the world is out there waiting for you. Peter Jennings is a high school dropout. There are so many people who don't have formal education who are multimillionaires. Why? Because of common sense. And because they really wanted it.

Fernando Mateo is Founder, Chairman, and CEO of Carpet Fashions, Inc. of New York City, a commercial carpet installation company. He grew up in New York City. He began selling furniture in high school and started Carpet Fashions when he was seventeen. In 1993, he and his son Fernando Mateo, Jr., conceived and implemented the "Toys for Guns" and "Goods for Guns" programs, which took four thousand guns off New York City streets, gained worldwide attention, and inspired similar efforts in many cities. He is now launching a new venture, Mateo Express, a money transfer service for customers in the United States, the Caribbean, and Latin America.

If you develop a chip on your shoulder, it can screw you up for life, and prevent you from achieving anything.

Dan Garcia
Senior Vice President
Warner Brothers

LIFE isn't always fair. I went to a Catholic school that was all Mexican kids in one of the poor sections of L.A. Later on I was bused to a school that was mostly all white kids. I was essentially an outcast. I didn't relate to anybody there, and they didn't relate to me, so I sat alone. It was really humiliating. I just withdrew, I was very quiet, and I felt sort of inferior. I mean, that's really how I felt.

It wasn't until I got in the army that I felt different, and what made me feel different there was I had three years of college under my belt. I was more educated than most of my officers. But that didn't make them assume that I was anything other than a moron, and it was interesting to watch how they treated me.

I was wounded in combat in Vietnam. I was sent back to my combat unit after having very significant chest wounds, like a punctured lung. On the operating table I was told I was being sent back to combat by a Texan doctor who was almost laughing. There was a huge eruption within the ward. Nurses came in yelling and screaming at the guy for being a racist. Things like that happen.

I wouldn't have gotten into UCLA had it not been for some sort of minority admission plan. I was just below the cut for a regular admit because you had to be in the 97th percentile, and I was in the 96th.

When I started looking for a job with a law firm, I can't count the number of times I walked into a room and looked around and realized that I was the only Latino in the room, probably the only Latino any of those people had ever seen. It was most pronounced the first couple of times I went to New York and I was young and had long hair and very dark skin. Those Wall Street law firms had never seen anything like me. Some people would smirk at me. But you know what? I lived through a war. By that time I wasn't exactly intimidated easily. I just ignored it. And I found over time that most people will come around.

You may have to grin and bear it for a while, but people after that will respond to the quality of your work—or the lack of quality of your work. That's been the lesson I've learned. So sometimes it's hard to take, but if you let it overcome you, then you get down on yourself, and you lose confidence and you don't perform.

You can turn them around with your performance.

Law firms aren't particularly communal, nurturing environments. I knew that. And one thing that distinguished me from a lot of lawyers was since the world hadn't treated me with enormous affection, I didn't go to my law firm thinking they were going to love me. It was a place to work. I didn't feel this need to be loved, and as a result, I treated it as a business. I didn't get hurt nearly as badly as a lot of my white friends who really suffered because they were forced to compete with each other. They weren't loved, they weren't number one in their class anymore. They were just a bunch of lawyers in a law firm and it was a rude comeuppance for them.

Dan Garcia is Senior Vice President of Warner Brothers in Burbank, California. He was raised in L.A.'s Crenshaw district, earned a bachelor's degree from Loyola University of Los Angeles, a master's degree from the University of Southern California, and a juris doctor from UCLA. He began his career at the Los Angeles law firm Munger, Tolls in 1974, was made partner in 1978, and worked there as a litigation trial lawyer through 1991, doing everything from real estate law to contracts and insurance. He joined Warner Brothers in 1991 and handles real estate and public affairs for the motion picture studio. As a U.S. Army platoon sergeant in Vietnam, he was wounded several times. He was also head of the Police Commission that suspended Los Angeles Police Commissioner Daryl Gates in 1991.

OFF THE RECORD

When I first encountered the reality of being different, I felt like a banana in Norway.

47-year-old executive vice president
of a Fortune 500 company

I got quite a rude welcome when I was assigned to a factory in Michigan. If I were in a court of law, I'm not sure I could prove it was because I was Latino, but being a foreigner, speaking with an accent, being different, with a Ph.D., I was a very atypical guy, and I was welcomed to that place like somebody welcomes cancer of the pancreas.

Until then I had lived in very, very protected environments, in a university, with people who spoke many languages, an ivory tower research center environment where I never really confronted the fact that I was different from anybody else.

I had been in the United States for probably ten years. I had never heard anybody call me a name that was derogatory in an ethnic sense. This was my first real-life situation. I was different, I was maybe even perceived as a threat. I heard all kinds of ethnic innuendos. It was a way of life there.

"What the hell are you doing here taking jobs from somebody else? Why don't you go back to your goddamn country where they need you?" Those were some of the remarks I heard. And it was one hell of an experience. Because then it really motivated me to excel, because I knew that the rules would not be the same for me. So, I worked twice as hard and was, in retrospect, very successful.

That very unwelcome welcome motivated me enormously. I wanted to prove myself and go the extra yard. I would not recommend to anybody that they be welcomed that way, but that sort of challenge really becomes a tremendous motivator. It did for me.

The familia *network can be a tremendous success asset.*

Adela Cepeda
President and Founder
AC Advisory

CAN I have a marriage, three children, and my own company? Of course it's possible.

Now, it isn't perfect. My house doesn't look the way I want it to look. There are crayon marks on furniture, there are crayon marks on the walls. There are three individuals who haven't developed all of the habits I'd like them to. But I have to let that go. I have to live with that.

There are times that are very, very crazy, when they have to be picked up, or the baby-sitter is out. But Latinas have a great advantage in this area, and I have benefited from it. We have families who accept the notion that when the younger generation works, the older generation helps out.

For example, my husband got sick last year. And my mother came to be with me. She and my father have never been separated, but she came. And it wasn't because I can't afford a housekeeper, but because people did it for her. My grandmother lived with us and raised us while my mother worked. And when my grandmother had to leave for something, an aunt came and stayed with us. I guess my mother felt now it was her turn to help me.

So, for Latina women, we can take advantage of the fabulous family support we have to help take care of our children. I had an aunt who lived with me for six years, taking care of my girls, and I provided support for her. She loves children, so everything to do with the children was her responsibility. And who better to take care of the children than *familia*?

Latinas have more challenges in our lives and that makes us stronger.

Ramona Martinez
Owner
Uniglobe Travel Agency

I do a lot of mentoring with young Latina students. I helped start the National Hispana Leadership Institute. And I am very impressed by the fact that most of the fellows are bilingual. They use their language for success. They bring so much determination and confidence to the table, particularly for small businesses. They need to know that they can do it, but that it's a lot of hard work and a lot of frustration, too.

A few years ago my sister and I decided to open our own travel agency. We were both married, and our children pretty well on their way. We told our husbands we wanted to buy this franchise and we were going to go to banks to put together our financial package. So we did, and everybody turned us down. Our husbands were very supportive. If they had said no, we would have done it anyway!

We were really upset with one particular institution where we had our checking accounts and everything. They just looked at us and told us that as two married women, they could not finance anything for us without our husband's signatures. So what we did was form a corporation, the four of us. And we were able to borrow the money to buy the franchise because we all had very good financials. There are still a lot of barriers in financial institutions for women who want to acquire their own businesses, especially if they have always filed joint income tax returns with their husbands. It's very difficult. We found a way.

The first couple of years were just as difficult. I never took a full salary. And it was very frustrating when I was the one doing the sales and marketing, to have a lot of doors closed in my face. The excuse was, "You have no experience in the business." That was the biggest letdown I had, trying to get as many customers as possible so we could start generating some revenue and build our business. It took a good two years.

My parents were totally shocked when we went into business. "For sure they'll never last a year," my mother said, and she probably would have been right if we hadn't been so determined. I've been able to make it a success because I've included my family. My sister is my partner. And I really think we Latinas are stronger than most people. First of all, we're female. Second of all, we're minority women. Latinas have more challenges to face, so by the time we go into business, we're ahead of the game.

Ramona Martinez is Owner of Uniglobe Travel Agency in Denver. She grew up near downtown Denver in a Mexican-American family that has been in Colorado for six generations, and worked for the Denver City Council. She and her sister started Uniglobe in 1986. She is a founder of the National Hispana Leadership Institute.

Latinas put limitations on themselves if they don't recognize how talented they are.

Marcela Donadio
Partner
Ernst & Young

COMING from Panama, not having grown up in an environment where there were real distinctions as to whether you were a minority or not, I never really understood what all that meant until I got here.

Don't put any limitations on yourself. A lot of my clients are taken aback when I say, "Oh, I'm from Panama." While I'm proud of my heritage, I don't feel I should either use it as a crutch or as leverage. It's a nonissue. I've accomplished what I have accomplished because of my personal skills and my abilities.

You can be successful and have a family. You have to be happy at home and you have to be happy at work. And you have to set priorities. Sometimes your family is going to be your first priority. And sometimes work is going to have to be a priority. You have to be able to recognize that. When you make that decision, you shouldn't feel guilty.

My husband tends to say that I think more like a man

than a woman. I don't know if that's true or not. In Panama many women have leadership positions and have worked all their lives. I went to an all-girls school when I was growing up, and I read recently that women who go to all-girls schools seem to do well in leadership because we don't have any of the limitations of having to worry about competing with the men.

≡≡≡≡≡≡≡≡≡≡

Being Latina is my greatest asset.

Nely Galan
President
Galan Entertainment
20th Century Fox

BEING Latina makes me journey-oriented versus goal-oriented. Being a Latina is totally a positive in business, because what it gives you is a soul. Our culture is journey-oriented, it's into loving the process. The way that orientation helps you in business is that it makes you be more open to different things. It makes you be soft, and it makes you listen to people.

It also allows you to be nurturing, because it all comes from a cultural place that allows you to have a failure. It's okay to be vulnerable and have a failure and be ambitious and hard-driving at the same time.

> *Latin culture is very matriarchal. People don't usually think of it that way, but it is. The women act like they're letting the men get their way, but they really get their way and they know their power as women. In business that's a big asset.*

I don't really believe in melding in with the paint. I think that life is about creating a unique persona, and using that unique persona to bring people into your world and make them think it's fun. I don't put on a persona, I don't try to be quiet, I don't try to be corporate, I don't try to wear an outfit that I would never wear. I try to be myself. It's only the people in life that are threatened by you that don't allow you to be you.

> *I think many Latinas are fearless. That's another success factor.*

I've actually had three friends call me and tell me they want me to teach them fearlessness. I don't think I'm really fearless. I'm very fearful about certain things. But I think that fearlessness comes from really feeling confidence in something. It's only the times when I don't feel confident about something that I remotely feel any sense of fear. Then I know I have to confront the fear in order to conquer it. I guess that's the part that's hardest for me: I'm afraid to be vulnerable.

There was a singular event that changed my life. It was when I was accused of plagiarism in high school. I wrote a paper that was so good that the nuns at my school decided I must have cheated. They called in my parents. The reason it hurt me so much was because my parents were involved. They were the thing I protected the most in life. That day, as my mother says, my metamorphosis occurred—from a saint to a beast. "You went from being a goody-two-shoes to a beast that has a big mouth and doesn't put up with anything," she said. I literally changed overnight. I really believe human beings are able to change overnight. I've seen it happen in my life.

It was an instant change. I remember what it felt like, and the next day I didn't feel like the same person. I had been victimized, and I decided I couldn't allow myself to be victimized one more day. I realized it doesn't pay to be a wimp. I find myself not feeling a lot of compassion for wimpiness, but I have to realize that I'm a former wimp myself!

Nely Galan is President of Galan Entertainment, a venture of 20th Century Fox in Los Angeles. She was born in Cuba, grew up in New Jersey, and started as an editorial assistant at *Seventeen* magazine at the age of seventeen. She hosted and produced a wide variety of TV productions for networks including HBO and E! before launching her current venture with Fox, designed to produce Latino motion picture and TV ventures in the United States and internationally.

Don't wait for things to be handed to you. You have to create your next job. Prove that you can do it and then go for it and say, "This is what I want for money and this is what I want for a title."

Esther Rodriguez
Vice President
General Instrument Corporation

HISPANIC women who are trying to make it in the United States should consider the fact that they have the good fortune to be both bilingual and bicultural. Use that as a positive. It has been one of my greatest assets.

> *Being a Latina is a tremendous business advantage.*

I started my career in Chicago with a consumer products company in international marketing. I always saw what the next opportunity was around me, and before anybody offered me a job, I created my next job. And that's the advice I have always given people who have worked with me.

When I was in Chicago I did exactly that. The person I was working for when I asked for the title and the money said, "But you are almost that." I said, "Yes, but almost doesn't count." I put my job on the line, and said, "Look, I know I can do better than this, either here or somewhere else. So I'm going to resign if what I need isn't met."

I had to take it to the last hour, and still my supervisor didn't think I was going to go through with it. I was already doing the job that I wanted to get compensated and recognized for. And I chose to look for other alternatives if I didn't get what I wanted. Finally I did get it.

> *When you see an opportunity, go do the job. And after you've proven that you know how to do it well, ask for the recognition. Very few people can argue with that. It's difficult to argue with results.*

I'll give you an example. I had the opportunity to go to Mexico City to promote one of our products, although Mexico City was not my area of responsibility. I met with a group of executives who composed the board of directors of the key companies in the cable industry in Mexico. Most of them were technical people, engineering backgrounds. I was able to explain to them, in Spanish and in a style that met their culture, what the benefits of our products were for their business. I walked out of that meeting with a contract, and I had created one of the best personal business relationships I have ever had.

So I came back with the contract. And the president of my company said, "You did what? You have that contract?"

"Yes, I have it," I said. "Here it is." Many of my peers who were in the Latin American business environment, but did not have the background or the culture that I have, had not succeeded there before.

The bottom line is that every one of the major media entities in Mexico has now adopted our technology. It's the country that has the largest number of our products outside of the United States. And now it has taken me to a landmark business arrangement with the Mexican government to create an educational satellite delivery network that will eventually reach 170,000 schools throughout the country.

The social impact that will have on the Mexican people is tremendous. And my being Latin and making our customers feel that they're dealing with someone who understands them and their needs have been tremendous assets for me and for the company.

Esther L. Rodriguez is Vice President, New Business Development, Satellite Systems for General Instrument Corporation in San Diego, and is an industry expert on the home satellite entertainment market, pay-per-view, and pay-TV marketing. From 1987 to 1992, she was general manager of G.I.'s Satellite Video Center. She was born in Cuba, graduated from the University of Havana, and began her career as an international marketing executive for Alberto-Culver Company in Chicago.

═══════════════

OFF THE RECORD

Latin men can be stereotyped as sexist when they're not.

**37-year-old president of a
manufacturing company**

ONE instance where being Latin was probably an obstacle for me was in an organization made up primarily of women. I was in New York at a seminar, and as we were walking back to the hotel, I made a very innocuous comment to a woman who was working with me. When she called me a "Latin chauvinist pig," my jaw dropped.

"I don't understand," I said.

"That was one of the most sexist things I ever heard," she said. "But, then again, I shouldn't expect anything less from a Latin."

I said, "Whoa." Then I turned the tables on her. "Well, look," I said, "I work for a Latin company, I come out of California, I'm Latin. So that's probably all you're ever going to hear from me."

It was amazing at the time because she had stereotyped me from the very start. She really expected me to be a chauvinist, sexist Latin Lothario type of person, and she found out later on that that was not me at all. That stereotype was standing in the way of our ability to build a camaraderie.

So I told her if that was who she thought I was, then no matter what I did or said, she was going to interpret it that way because of my background.

You always have to be careful in situations like that because people are going to stereotype you, or at least have a preconceived notion about you, obviously because of who you are and if you have a surname that doesn't happen to be "white." I could have gone to war with her but I chose to defuse it and to make her an ally. From that point on, she and I became the best of friends.

INSIGHT 4

IMAGE

For Latinos, image is crucial. Never underestimate the "passive" side of success. How you are perceived and how things are articulated can be as important as substance.

How you are perceived and how things are articulated are sometimes more important than the content of what you're saying. That is an obstacle we Hispanics need to be aware of.

José Ofman
Vice President and Group Executive
EDS

THINGS are often as they are perceived, not necessarily as they really are. For Hispanics, there are significant cultural differences that, because of how we grew up, we're not aware of how they impact non-Hispanic people. For example, if English is your second language, and your grammar is not appropriate, I don't care how intelligent or how good your idea is, it's not going to be perceived as a good idea.

Having an accent is part of my life, but writing incorrectly is not. I can do something about it. I have seen many ideas be presented by two or three people, and bought strictly on the basis of who presented them best.

Sensitivity to the culture and awareness of cultural differences is something we need to work at. Hispanics can be very much "in-your-face" types of people when we discuss things. We get very close to the other person, our voice gets louder than that of most Anglos, and a lot of us are not as aware of the impact that has.

Look, if I said to you that being Hispanic is irrelevant, that would be stupid. People absorb the overall picture that you present, and being different is usually a barrier, and definitely I was different. It was an obstacle I had to overcome. Luckily enough, I was in the kind of company that is a meritocracy to the nth degree. That's why I'm still here, twenty-three years later. The only way you get ahead here is by merit.

José Ofman is Vice President and Group Executive of EDS in Plano, Texas, formerly a subsidiary of General Motors. He received a bachelor's degree in mechanical engineering from the University of the Andes in Colombia, bachelor of science and master of science degrees in mechanical engineering from the University of Pittsburgh, and joined EDS in 1972.

OFF THE RECORD

Do I have "affirmative action" stamped on my head?

32-year-old marketing executive

THE odds are that most white guys have not had meaningful connections (in the business sense) with many Latinos yet. The way they behave sometimes makes me wonder. They'll say: "You don't have an accent or anything." "You work hard." What the hell does that mean? "Articulate." I've been called articulate by so many interviewers. Out of forty interviews in college I heard "articulate" twenty times. I'm not kidding. And when someone says, "Boy, you know, you work really hard," I wonder, "Are you surprised?"

Of course I work really hard. I wouldn't be here if I didn't work really hard. But I wonder how often that is said of white guys. I've never been a white guy in an interview. But I've asked them, and no one reports being told, "You're so articulate. You don't have an accent. You work really hard." You're glad they recognize these qualities in you, and that you are rebutting their presumptions, but you also think, "Oh, God, you mean you assumed I was going to be inarticulate and lazy?" It's really scary!

I do make some decisions emotionally, and I think that's perfectly valid. If I don't have a gut sense about something, I'm certainly not going to do it. But that's considered irrational, emotional, female, Latin. If you disagree or argue on something, it's a "Latin temper." One time in a board meeting, I was arguing about a budget issue when this guy said to me, "Uh-oh, watch that Latin temper." I wasn't yelling. What do you do to reclaim your authority when someone says that? My solution was to joke about it. I laughed and said, "You're a smart man if you learn to fear me now!"

I don't want to burn those bridges too quickly. My bridges are tougher to build, so I'm not going to torch them.

For Latinos and African-Americans, image is especially crucial. Never underestimate the "passive" side of success.

David Morales
President
Latin America
Scientific Atlanta

IBM taught me that image was very important. How you looked, how you presented yourself, who you associated yourself with—all were very important.

> *There's an active component to success and there's a passive component to success. You need both to truly be successful long-term.*

The work you do is the active component of success. The passive component includes presenting the right image of yourself, the way you dress, the way you talk, who you associate with.

Never underestimate the passive side of success. The guys at IBM who tried to buck the system got in trouble. For example, the company was real big on white button-down oxford shirts and wing tips. The mavericks who didn't really adhere to that had a rougher time of it, especially if they didn't have results to back themselves up.

Image is important, especially for a minority person. You've got to give people reasons to find common ground with you. That's fundamental. You've got to look the part, you've got to act the part, and then you've got to perform.

You can never become one of the "good old boys." Never forget where you come from. Accommodate without compromising your integrity.

Israel Bulbank
President and CEO
Unalite Electric and Lighting Corporation

THE most important assets to bring to the table are honesty, integrity, and trust. You should never forget where you come from or who you are, no matter what you're doing at the time. You have to learn how things are done, and accommodate without compromising your own integrity. It's a very, very fine line to walk.

You may want to distance yourself from many things that happen in business. You draw the line. For example, people will let you know that you have to do certain things to get their business. But if they are against your grain or against your integrity, if it's not the proper way of doing business, just don't do it.

I've seen many people make the wrong ethical choices, and within a few years, their business fails because it does not stand on solid ground.

Israel Bulbank is President and CEO of Unalite Electric and Lighting Corporation in Long Island City, New York. He was born in Cuba, attended New York University, worked for an import-export company, and also served in the U.S. Army and as a lighting company executive before heading up Unalite in 1976.

===

People who come from ethnic backgrounds want to be taken seriously in their professional lives. And that's good. But don't overdo it.

Antonio Rodriguez
Senior Vice President
Seagram Spirits and Wine Group

SOMETIMES "minorities" are so intent on doing the right thing and being seen as professional, and not fitting the stereotypes—lazy, flippant, or whatever—that they take themselves too seriously. Remember to be human, remember to be warm. These are success factors too—being able to deal with people.

I think if you asked my boss about me, he'd say my technical skills are good, but it's my people relations skills that make the difference. They are more important than my education and everything else. They make the real difference. If I'm ever going to be president of a company and lead people, it won't be because of my Princeton degree. It's the ability to motivate people and work with them that really counts. And to do that you can't be an iceberg. You've got to laugh with them once in a while. You've got to be able to take your tie off. You've got to be able to invite them to your house and relate to them. You know their family, they know your family.

Sense of humor is very important in business in general, regardless of where you come from. But you also have to know when to express it. Especially in my area, finance, people expect you to be boring. If I get their attention with a little joke at the right time, it can make it easier for them to understand what I'm talking about and I keep their interest. But you've also got to know when not to joke.

When I interview some people, they come across like Joe Harvard Business School, so intense and so serious. I'm not saying you have to crack jokes left and right during the interview. But if people don't have a human side to them, in this company at least, they tend to have a short-lived career regardless of how good their résumés are. We're more effective when we enjoy working with each other, because then the ideas start to flow.

===

Hispanics should say what they think and be assertive. Intellectual honesty works every time.

Emilio Alvarez-Recio
Vice President, Global Advertising
Colgate-Palmolive Company

In our Hispanic culture there is a tendency to want to be kind, to want to please, to want to help. But our desire to please and to do the right thing for people is sometimes confused with servility, or lack of assertiveness, or not having one's own thoughts about some matter, when nothing could be further from the truth.

> *It is important to be assertive, it is important to say what you honestly think and let the chips fall where they may.*

The best armor that you can have in business is creating a reputation for being intellectually honest, and for expressing yourself well. If you combine that with being smart and working very hard, then you have a winning proposition.

Emilio Alvarez-Recio is Vice President, Global Advertising for Colgate-Palmolive Company in New York City, a global consumer products company. He joined Colgate in 1967 and has held senior marketing and operations posts for the company in the United States, Europe, Asia, Spain, the Middle East, and Latin America, including president of the North America division, president of Colgate-Palmolive Spain, and president of Colgate-Palmolive Philippines. He is also a member of the board of directors of NatWest Bank. He was born in Cuba, attended law school at Havana University, and began his career in marketing at Richardson-Vicks.

Don't be afraid to be the champion of something you strongly believe in.

Dr. Pedro Cuatrecasas
President of Research
Parke-Davis

DON'T take it personally when your ideas are turned down. Reexamine them and reintroduce them in a way that will get more support. For example, I was involved in developing a promising new drug that our business people didn't think would be profitable. I kept working with them and explaining how strong the product would be, and now it is a billion-dollar business.

I quickly become excited about other people's work. Enthusiasm is contagious, and a powerful attribute to inspire other people—your interest in them, in their work, asking questions, listening well, and encouraging them to try new things.

Dr. Pedro Cuatrecasas is President of Research for Parke-Davis, a major pharmaceutical company located in Ann Arbor, Michigan. He obtained bachelor's and doctor of medicine degrees at Washington University, performed his internship and residency in clinical medicine at Johns Hopkins University, and worked at the National Institutes of Health, Burroughs Wellcome, and Glaxo before joining Parke-Davis. He has authored over four hundred original scientific publications.

===

Know when to take a stand.

J. Armando Ramirez
Senior Vice President
National City Corporation

IF you do good work, I think eventually you'll be recognized. But if you think something should be done, state it. And back it up. It's easy to analyze something forever and never reach a decision. At some point you need to say, "Okay, I know all I need to know and this is what I recommend."

J. Armando Ramirez is Senior Vice President, Mergers and Acquisitions, for National City Corporation in Cleveland.

===

Quantify your results.

Dan Gomez
President
Bell Atlantic Directory Graphics

I learned early on that in a job, if I could produce results and actually quantify those results to people, I got more opportunity. You have to make sure that you are seen, and you have to make sure that you tell people that you directly contributed in some tangible way. That doesn't mean you have to grandstand. You need to be a team player as well.

Dan Gomez is President of Bell Atlantic Directory Graphics in Norristown, Pennsylvania, a division of Bell Atlantic Corporation. He was born in Topeka, Kansas, grew up in Springfield, Virginia, earned a bachelor's degree in economics at Wharton, and an MBA at the Virginia Polytechnic Institute and State University.

OFF THE RECORD

I was labeled the token Latino.

**43-year-old division president of a
computer services company**

I'VE never avoided or overplayed my ethnic background.
But one time it was overplayed for me when the company
did an annual report focusing on the people who worked
there. The theme of the report was "Diversity." The first guy
featured was the only really senior-level black executive.
The second one was me. The third one was a woman from
another division. As one of my friends said, the only thing
missing was a Japanese lesbian. Originally, when I was interviewed they said, "Oh, we want you in the annual report
because you're the youngest vice president." Instead I was
labeled the "token Latino."

I think that's bullshit. We are going to screw our own people if we apply some kind of quota system. Because then I'll
never be able to do what I do today, which is walk into my
office and know I'm there because of my abilities. If you've
got people looking over our shoulders saying we're there because of some quota, you're going to take away our pride.

Yes, you want to make sure people have an opportunity to
develop and get exposure. But if you push it too far into
boxes, you've blown it. You've blown it not just for them, but
for everybody else.

They are many more women and people from ethnic
backgrounds in top positions today. But my CEO knows
business is so tough that if he doesn't have the best, he's
going to lose, because the politically correct report card is
not going to matter much with his earnings per share.
That's how it works.

When Ivy League schools didn't admit women, they were
looking at only half the applicant pool. They missed the

whole point. Now that they've opened up, they've got a better overall pool, because the bottom half of the male pool before was not as smart as the top half of the female pool. So now you've got the best of everything.

Business is the same way. I say "open it up," as opposed to "require." No one says we have to have 50 percent women. Open it up to the best applicants and then let's see what the ratios are. If it ends up being 90 percent Latino, that's fine. I know this sounds idealistic, but that's the whole point. That's what diversity should be about.

Be strong on the issues—pero suave con la gente! (but soft on the people)

Luis Lamela
CEO and President
CAC-United HealthCare Plans of Florida

THE turning point of my career came in 1988. My company is an HMO serving South Florida, including Little Havana, and we were losing money. We were bought by the Ramsay Group, an Australian firm, and they found out after they bought us that we had more problems than they thought.

The Australians came in to talk to the senior officers of the company, and everybody was scared that they were going to fire all of us. Being the Latin that I am, I was very excited and upset. My hands were all over the place. They looked at me and said, "Luis, relax, we just want to talk to you."

"I am relaxed!" I said. "This is as relaxed as I get!" Then I said, "Listen, I'm very upset because I thought a company like the Ramsay Group, which has done this, this, and this"—and I went through all the things they had done that I had read about—"I thought we were going to be focused and disciplined and attack our problems."

"And you know what? When I thought I saw the light at the end of that tunnel, it was the light of an oncoming train full of more disorganization and more BS! You guys don't know what you're doing!"

The next day I was supposed to go on a vacation. My mother's dream was to go to Paris and I had saved money to take her there. People said, "What? Are you crazy? You're going to leave in the middle of this?"

It turned out that Mr. Paul Ramsay, the chairman of the Ramsay Group, loved that because he is truly a family person. He said, "We know you're leaving on vacation, but can you stop telling us what's wrong and tell us how to fix it?"

"Oh, you think that's all that's wrong?" I said. "Let me tell you more!" I'd been there for ten years and I really knew what was wrong everywhere. My ideas were no different than what I told the previous management. We just never implemented them.

> *Sometimes people spend too much time trying to say what they think the other person wants to hear.*

I am soft with people, but I'm very, very strong on the issues. I tell people the truth. And so I went on and on, pounding the table. They were taking notes and I was going full speed ahead. Finally, they asked me to put my ideas in writing so they could study them while I was on vacation.

I got a call from the Australians when I was in Paris. They told me they had decided to leave an Australian as president of the company and I would report to him. Instead of being fired, I got promoted.

When I got back, I told them what was needed to turn the company around. "We have to retrench," I said. "It's not going to get better. It's going to get worse, and it's going to take time." So we retrenched. I told them it would take eighteen months to turn it around, but it only took fourteen. We reorganized and built a foundation, and from June of 1989 until today every month has been profitable. For three years in a row we've been one of *Fortune* magazine's 100 fastest-growing companies in the United States and in 1994 we merged with United HealthCare Corp., *Fortune* magazine's most admired health care company in America.

> *Never give up, no matter what. You can fall down a million times. Just keep going!*

Be sensitive to people, understand what they need and don't need, and especially take the time to educate them about the important issues and how they can be addressed. Don't deviate from the issues. But take your time with the people.

Luis Lamela is CEO and President of CAC-United HealthCare Plans of Florida in Coral Gables, a company that has the distinction of being the first licensed HMO in the state, celebrating twenty-five years of serving the Florida community. He was born in Camagüey, Cuba, graduated from the University of Florida with a BS in pharmacy, and earned a master's in business administration from the University of Miami. He started his career as pharmacy manager for Treasury Pharmacy, joined Ramsay as director of pharmacy in 1974, and rose through the ranks to become CEO in 1992.

The biggest mistake people working for me can make is to knock on my door, come into my office and ask me, "What do you want me to do?"

Hector Ruiz
Executive Vice President and General Manager
Paging Products Group, Motorola Inc.

IT is a real weakness if you can't come up with your own ideas and present them.

Gather the level of authority you think is necessary for

whatever task you have to do. You've got to take risks and you are going to have some setbacks. Don't underestimate that. That's to be expected and embraced.

No matter at what level in the organization you are, assume a certain role. Don't let somebody tell you what your role is. Assume it. Take into account what people expect of you, but go ahead and assume a role that you think makes sense.

Also remember that Latinos have a built-in business advantage—cultural sensitivity.

Hector Ruiz is Executive Vice President and General Manager of the Paging Products Group of Motorola Inc. in Boynton Beach, Florida, overseeing worldwide operations of Motorola's paging businesses. He grew up in a Mexican-American family in Texas, earned bachelor's and master's degrees in electrical engineering from the University of Texas at Austin, and a doctorate from Rice University. He joined Motorola in 1977 as operations manager in the firm's semiconductor group. He is a Director of the Hispanic Engineer National Achievement awards.

Know when to give a quick answer and when to say, "Well, I think the answer is this, but we need to verify it."

Ed Gonzalez
Partner
Skadden, Arps, Slate, Meagher & Flom

In the practice of law an awful temptation is triggered by clients who want to have instant answers. But at the end of the day, the most important thing is to be right. You don't have to have all the answers instantly when you're working in a complicated area. Sometimes a measured response is best. But you also have to recognize that you're dealing, at least in my field, in a business environment, so you don't have all day to come up with the answers. It's a balancing act.

Edward E. Gonzalez is Partner at the Skadden, Arps, Slate, Meagher & Flom law firm in Los Angeles. He handles the tax aspects of a variety of transactions, including mergers and acquisitions, U.S. and non-U.S. financial instruments, leveraged buyouts, debt restructurings, asset-based financings, tax controversies, and leveraged leases. He has advised both investment banks and corporations in the structuring of various acquisitions, financings, and refinancings, including Carr-Gottstein Properties, Inc., Price/Costco, Occidental Petroleum Corporation, Turner Broadcasting System, Inc., The Walt Disney Company, and Merrill Lynch & Co. He earned an A.B. from Princeton University (*summa cum laude*, Phi Beta Kappa), and a J.D. from Columbia University.

Our culture's respect and deference can be mistaken for a lack of confidence.

Andres V. Gil
Partner
Davis Polk & Wardwell

IN the Latino culture generally we are much more deferential, particularly to people who are older and people who are in authority. That's how I was brought up. You basically don't directly challenge older people, or people who are your direct superiors. You're taught to respect your elders.

The first day I arrived at my law firm, I called everybody "Mister," especially the partners. Finally, one of them said to me, "Please stop calling me Mister." And I realized after a while that my culturally ingrained deference was being mistaken for a lack of confidence or knowledge.

I learned another important lesson from working with somebody here who is much more aggressive, the sort of person who walks into a room and takes over. At times, watching him, I'd want to crawl under the table because I thought, "God, this guy is really going to set people on edge." But I noticed that most of the time he ended up having the center chair and was able to set the agenda for everybody else. It wasn't abrasive, it was a way of making his voice heard.

You can have that voice when you've done your homework and you know what you're talking about. I certainly could not do it the way he did it. I couldn't walk into a room in the same brash and abrupt way and take over. But, there were other ways that suited me better, not by being abrasive, but by having a well-researched point of view and showing people I'd done my homework.

In Latino culture I think the hierarchy is generally based on waiting your turn. When you get old enough, people will respect you and you will be pushed along. I see a lot of that in Latin America. But American culture is different. If you take the attitude of wait your turn, you'll never get it.

Andres V. Gil is a Partner of the Davis Polk & Wardwell law firm in New York City, specializing in securities offerings, privatizations, and cross-border acquisitions, joint ventures, and securities regulation. He was admitted to the New York Bar in 1982 and Conseil Juridique in France in 1985. He is a member of the Inter-American and International Bar Associations and is a director of the Puerto Rican Legal Defense and Education Fund. He was born in Cuba, graduated from Princeton University and the New York University School of Law, and joined Davis Polk in 1980 as a summer associate.

━━━━━━━━━━

When you're down, fight hard and don't get a bad attitude. Because then you lose twice.

Felix Rivera
Vice President
Johnson & Johnson Consumer Products Company

ONE of the toughest times in my career occurred in 1988–89, when there were two Johnson & Johnson plants in Puerto Rico. I was working in one and the other one was a small operation. And both plants reported to the same plant manager. Then management decided to remove that plant manager from the operation and split up the two plants. There would be two plant managers: one big job with five hundred people and a smaller job with ninety people. I thought I was the best qualified candidate for the big job. I ended up getting the smaller one.

It was very frustrating because I had really spent a lot of time in that big operation. And when I didn't get that job, I took it personally. I was a very hard-headed guy with the people who worked for the company stateside. I was a very tough person in the plant and I defended my values. And I probably didn't get the bigger job because they wanted a person who was a better team player. I thought a team player meant just doing what they wanted me to do. Sometimes they didn't have the right answers, and I was a bit tough on the U.S. management. I didn't have the image of being a good team player.

When I didn't get the bigger job, my initial reaction was "Oh, to hell with this company." But then I decided to show them what I could do, and do the best job possible. I worked my butt off on the ninety-person job, and two years later a new vice president of operations came in. He looked at the situation and he then asked me to run those two plants and one more on the island. So, two and a half years later I ended up running the little plant, the big plant, and a new plant that we had acquired.

In your lowest moments, don't react negatively to the company and say, "Oh, how unfair these people are." You have to look at the situation and either move on or work harder.

Corporate cultures can both stigmatize and place unrealistic expectations on Hispanics.

Don Flores
Publisher and Editor
The El Paso Times

SOME of the best fights in the business world are now occurring in glass skyscrapers and corporate boardrooms, away from cameras and reporters, where we Latinos are slowly making our way in and lobbying for more influence. However, if you spend too much of your time being an activist, you can lose the credibility of being a total manager. You're just talking about one issue, and you become a one-issue kind of manager. On the other hand, if you're not being an activist, then maybe you're not Hispanic enough. Some people may say, "Oh, you're a conformist. You've sold out."

In the newspaper business, our Hispanic readers expect us to be very Hispanic and our non-Hispanic readers will say, "Hey, how come we've got all this Hispanic stuff in our paper? Aren't we in America?"

> *There are expectations placed on you from both sides. In some cases there's no way you can meet them all, and it can drive you crazy.*

Some days I manage it well and some days not. I try to keep it in balance, and know that if I've got people at both extremes pulling at me, then I'm probably doing a good job. But there are other days when I go home wishing I were in Butte, Montana, where being Hispanic would not be an issue.

Being Hispanic in El Paso is different from being Hispanic in South Texas, which is different from being Hispanic in Washington or New York or in Los Angeles. I'm learning more about myself being here than I did in Iowa City. And it's good for me because it's fleshing out who I am—a Flores with a rich history. I grew up poor in a house that didn't have running water, had parents who weren't high school graduates but appreciated education, and I worked hard to get where I am today. I can go to schools and talk about that. I can relate to kids going through the same thing. "I've been there. I did that. And I made it." That's what I can give back to a community.

> *In some companies they expect Hispanics to act just like an Ivy Leaguer who has ten, fifteen years' experience—very aggressive, challenging, projecting ourselves as much as possible. In reality, many of the Hispanic managers I've worked for are reserved. They're not self-promoters, and come across as maybe not that excited. That can be a stigma. Hell, we're excited. It's just a different culture.*

At times I've been asked, "Can you be a little bit more aggressive?"

Well, I'm probably the most aggressive person there is when it's day in and day out. But in corporate meetings or sessions with a lot of other people, that's not you on stage, and some people feel uncomfortable trying to create a stage for themselves.

Hispanics have this stigma that we're not as outgoing and aggressive as we should be in the so-called mainstream culture. If so, a big part of the problem is that we work in corporate cultures that don't always embrace the differences we bring to the table.

Don Flores is Publisher and Editor of *The El Paso Times*, a Gannett daily newspaper located in El Paso, Texas. He earlier served in management and editorial positions at *The Iowa City Press-Citizen*, *The Tucson Citizen*, *The New Mexican*, and *The Dallas Morning News*. He was born in Goliad, Texas, graduated from the Southwest Texas State University in San Marcos, and started out as a sports editor at *The San Marcos Daily Record*. He has served as president of the National Association of Hispanic Journalists and as a Pulitzer Prize jurist, and serves on the Task Force on Minorities in the Newspaper Business of the American Newspaper Publishers Association.

========

The Latino value of humility can be a powerful tool for success.

Frank Alvarez
Vice President
Kaiser Foundation

A headhunter once called me and said, "Can we get together for lunch?" In a weak moment I gave in. And after we had talked an hour about who I was and what I did, she said, "You know, you don't sell yourself very well." "What do you mean?" I said. And she said, "Why don't you talk about the great days that you've had, or the huge successes?" "That's a good question," I told her.

What the headhunter was saying was "If you want to succeed, you've got to be able to blow your own horn." It's very hard for me to do that. I guess I'll never be the head of a Fortune 500 company, because I don't know how to say "I."

Because of our culture, many Latinos are taught to value humility and not to talk about ourselves. But you can also go too far in the other direction. I was once being considered for a promotion. I was doing a good job, my numbers were good, and in the interviews for the position, I came in underprepared. I'd been in the organization long enough, and I thought I had a reputation for being a success. I fell flat on my face. I was awful. I was acting cocky and confident, because I thought that was what they wanted. I didn't get the job.

They brought in an outsider, a person who knew nothing about the way we do business. For me it was a double hit—the rejection of not getting the position, and then having to train somebody from the outside to be my boss. All of these emotions came flooding to the surface, things like "I don't belong here. I'm going to get the hell out. I'm going to do other things." It was probably the most personally difficult time of my career because I felt devalued.

I finally realized what had gone wrong. They wanted to

feel involved. I wanted to feel independent. My numbers were okay but they thought, "Alvarez is a maverick. We want an interaction, and he isn't giving us that." And I thought they were going to value me for being a maverick.

I had to swallow my pride big-time, and for two years I dedicated myself to helping my new boss be a success and changing my management style, asking for advice from corporate headquarters instead of being on my own. So two years passed, there was a major reorganization, and I interviewed for another major promotion. This time I prepared carefully for the interviews, including the final interview with the regional manager, who was my boss's boss.

"I want you to know that the last two years have been an important learning opportunity for me," I said. "I haven't given my best yet. And I'd really like the opportunity to do that. We've got to work together. And I think I can do that."

The CEO said, "Frank, I've watched you change for two years, and I've heard other people say you've changed. This is a real transformation. I don't know how the hell you did it, but you've got the job."

I was able to rewrite the "book" that had been written on me. The "I" is what I had used the first time, thinking that was what they wanted. The "we" was what they were really looking for.

You've got to find people who are not willing to feather your nest, people who will tell you the truth instead of what they think you want to hear.

Humility was a decisive factor in my success.

Frank D. Alvarez recently served as Vice President of Kaiser Foundation in San Francisco, a national managed care organization. He was born and raised in East Los Angeles in a Mexican-American family, attended East Los Angeles Junior College, and received a master's degree in public health from the University of California at Berkeley. Mr. Alvarez was winner of the 1994 César Chávez Award from the California Chicano/Latino Inter-Segmental Convocation, and is chairperson of the board for the National Hispanic Scholarship Fund.

We're great entrepreneurs, we just have to learn how to sell ourselves better and not be afraid to ask for the order.

Adela Cepeda
President and Founder
AC Advisory

LATINOS are extremely loyal. That's why we're not always the best salespeople. Because we're so loyal, I would give my business to you because you're a Latino and I know you, and my parents know you and all that. And I assume that since you know what I do, if you ever want somebody to manage your money, you're going to call me. I don't have to make a sales pitch to you. It's almost part of the extended-family concept. If we know each other, we don't make the calls. We don't sell. It's not part of our culture.

Our native countries are oligarchical. A handful of guys and families may sell among each other, but they do it all themselves, and nobody breaks in. So why are you going to sell to one of those guys? He's rich, he knows your family, he wouldn't have an interest. It would be embarrassing, so you don't do it.

We have to get beyond that. One thing Smith Barney taught me was to make sales calls. And it was a great experience. We have to be taught to sell, even to people who know us. In my case, maybe it hasn't occurred to them that I could manage their IRA. But we are culturally inhibited from "promoting ourselves," and it is something we should try to change.

On the other hand, we're fabulous entrepreneurs. A man once told me that entrepreneurship is genetic, and that people in certain parts of the world don't have it. If he ever crossed the border to Mexico, he would see just how entrepreneurial we are. We're the kind of people who, if we get enough money to buy a blender, we don't just have it at home sitting there. We'd be out selling *batidos* on the corner. Then we're freezing *granizados* in the refrigerator, making money from the refrigerator and the blender. And everybody's kids come by after school because they know we sell home-made *granizados*.

OFF THE RECORD

I was actually mistaken for the chauffeur.

**43-year-old division president
of a computer services company**

My success at an early age was my own worst enemy, especially working overseas. In New York it's not a big deal. There are a lot of young guys doing well, especially on Wall Street. So people are used to it. But when I went to London at the age of twenty-nine as the senior vice president of the biggest division of my company, the people there thought, "Who's this Spanish kid?"

My name didn't help. In Europe, southern Europeans tend to have the worst jobs, especially in London. They're stereotyped as the guys who clean up the office at night. The chauffeur Manuel was a very nice man from Salamanca, and I was actually mistaken several times for him, because we had the same last name. People would call my office and ask my secretary if I could drive somebody to the airport. She would be shocked.

I took it in stride. "I'm having a rough day here in finance," I told her one afternoon. "A ride to Heathrow might not be a bad idea. Tell Manuel to come up here and sit in my office. How much could he blow in an hour? Get me the keys to the Bentley and I'll drive."

In fact, the first day I showed up in London the same thing happened. I went in to the office of the European headquarters and said, "I'm here to see the president of the division." I gave the receptionist my name and she said, "Are you related to Manuel the chauffeur?"

If you get too upset, you walk around with a chip on your shoulder, and I've seen too many people like that. I would encourage Latinos to just relax a little bit because some people expect us to have a chip on our shoulder. And it's only going to hold you back.

The way you handle criticism is very important and it tells a lot about you. People watch the way you handle it. Don't get too defensive or emotional.

Sara Martinez Tucker
National Vice President
AT&T

WE Hispanics have a lot of pride in our work. I was always taught, "Don't brag about your work. Let your work speak for you." So it's hard for me to separate my personality or my sense of well-being from the work that I do. When my work gets criticized, I take it as a personal criticism. That's one of the reasons I get defensive easily. I've seen that in a lot of other Hispanics I work with.

> *Don't get defensive when you are criticized. Sit back and realize they're talking about your work, not you. Learn what you can from their input. They may not be right, but they're seeing it from a different perspective and you should try to be objective.*

Ask questions like "What's missing for you? What would make it work for you?" Try to turn criticism into a positive. Above all, you can't get too emotional. Other people probably manage that better than I do. I wear my heart on my sleeve. And many Hispanics that I work with, male and female, have a lot of emotion. Try to control it. As much as it's inherent in us, it can make others feel uncomfortable.

You have to control your ego.

Jorge Diaz
Vice President and Deputy Program Manager
Northrop Grumman Corp. B-2 Division

SOME people think that because they finished college, they're the greatest and the world owes them something.

College gives you a little key that opens a little box with a little bit of knowledge. And the first thing you have to learn is the size of your own ego.

> *You have to divorce yourself from the idea that somebody owes you something.*

Some of my peers had goals that were so ambitious and so unachievable that they made themselves very unhappy when they didn't achieve them. One wanted to be a CEO of a corporation at thirty-five. Now he's thirty-five and he's still a second-level manager. The first thing he should have done was get into a small company or create his own business with a few employees; then he could have become the CEO. There are a lot of opportunities to do that.

Don't set yourself unachievable goals. Don't see yourself as the greatest thing going. When I arrived in this country I didn't even understand the language. That was a humbling experience and it pushed me to learn some lessons quickly. The most important one was that an oversized ego will be an obstacle to success.

═══════════════

A major cause of failure for someone in power is arrogance.

Roman Martinez
Managing Director
Lehman Brothers

Whenever I have seen arrogance setting in, I know that some failure or setback will inevitably follow. You become arrogant when you think you're better than everybody else. And you can become arrogant toward the people you're managing or toward your clients. Whether it's in a person or a company, arrogance leads to setbacks or failure, because you get careless.

> *When you start thinking you're better than everybody else, or infallible, or indispensable, that's when your risks start increasing dangerously.*

We're all human, and there are many factors that go into success, including external factors you cannot control. Once you become arrogant your defenses are lowered simply because you think you don't need them. I am aware from personal experience of a situation involving a major financial services institution that had to be taken over by another firm where the CEO's arrogance led to his downfall. He thought he was infallible and could run the place by himself. He was wrong.

Roman Martinez IV is Managing Director of Lehman Brothers, a publicly held investment banking firm based in New York City. He was born in Cuba, earned a bachelor's degree from Boston College, and an MBA from the Wharton School of the University of Pennsylvania. He joined Kuhn Loeb & Co., a predecessor company, in 1971, and became a Managing Director in 1978. His experience includes helping to restructure Westinghouse Electric, Reed International, and Grupo Industrial Alfa, the acquisition of General Foods by Philip Morris, and the first public stock offering of Coca-Cola Enterprises.

Some people expect they're owed more than others because they're Hispanic or black or a woman. I think that is the kiss of death.

Emilio Alvarez-Recio
Vice President, Global Advertising
Colgate-Palmolive Company

THE moment you start expecting special treatment because of your race, sex, or ethnic origin, you generate nothing but the opposite of what you want to generate, including and most fervently from people like yourself. The last thing I want to see is a Hispanic trying to take unfair advantage of being a Hispanic. It really always backfires on you.

You may get to one level, but then you hit a ceiling, which is exactly what you don't want. You also create a very negative atmosphere for other Hispanics who aren't asking for any special treatment. If somebody gets to where he is just because he is Hispanic, people begin to wonder if any Hispanic person is really worth a damn. Hispanics are just as intelligent and as hardworking as anybody else, and that's the last thing we need.

Do your thing and be proud of who you are, but in a very positive, contributory way.

INSIGHT 5

NEVER FEAR
FAILURE

Accountability, vulnerability, and integrity are crucial success factors.

*I'm not afraid of failing, nor am I afraid of suc-
ceeding, which is a problem for some people. I
just like challenges.*

Jellybean Benitez
Chairman & CEO
Jellybean Productions, Inc.

I was born in Spanish Harlem, my parents are from Puerto
Rico, and I grew up in the South Bronx. I really came from
nothing, from a really poor family, a broken home. I didn't
have anyone I could trust, except my mother, who was very
supportive of me.

> *My mom would say all kinds of things that I still
> live by today: "If you don't ask you don't get."
> "Trust your instincts and don't be afraid to fail. The
> worst that can happen is that you'll learn some-
> thing from it."*

Drugs were really scary for me, because growing up in
that environment I saw lots of kids who were my age and by
the time they were twelve or thirteen were junkies, dead
from drugs, or in jail. But a tough neighborhood can actually be a good education for life. You're learning to survive.
You're fighting all the odds. It really taught me a lot of
things about life and my ability to survive and to believe in
myself.

Music was part of the culture I grew up in. I had a big
record collection. When my friends had parties I would sit
by the turntable and play my records for fear that they

would get stolen or scratched. My friends called me a dee-jay, but I was just changing records. What they were talking about was a club deejay.

The first time they took me to a club, I saw people were buying drinks for the deejay and all these pretty girls were coming up and asking for the names of songs. I thought, "This is my job! Free drinks, girls, yeah, I think I like this!"

I dropped out of high school. I always felt I was smarter than everyone else in my class—street-smart. I was very lucky and I had a plan. Dropping out of high school was a choice that I made, and based on all the negative forces around me, had I not dropped out I probably wouldn't be here today. So, for me it worked, but it worked because I had a plan. It wasn't like I said, "I'm out of here." I was already planning how I was going to get to college. I wasn't leaving anything to chance.

I was guaranteed to go to a city university, being a minority and having a high school equivalency diploma. So I went to Bronx Community College, and then I transferred to Baruch College. Then I transferred to the New School for Social Research. Education was important to me, even though I was already making more money as a deejay than I could ever generate from any career that I could think of.

In the Bronx everyone had a nickname. That way, if somebody did something wrong, everybody on the street would know who did it, but the police wouldn't. My sister always said to me, "Know what I mean, Jellybean?" because my initials are J.B. I wanted a deejay name that people would remember, as opposed to Deejay Joe Smith, so I became Jellybean. Its been my brand name ever since.

I was working in clubs in the Bronx, but what I really wanted to do was to work in Manhattan. So I got this *Cue* magazine, and looked up all the places that had clubs or dancing and called them all up and said, "I heard you were looking for a deejay." And they said, "We're not."

"Well, what happens if your deejay gets sick?" I said. "Oh, well, let me get your number." I said, "I'd like to audition.

Can I bring you a tape?" Just to get me off the phone they'd say, "Okay, send us a tape." I said, "I'm going to be in the neighborhood later, so I'll just drop it off."

Once I got there, I'd say, "Your deejay starts at ten o'clock. Why don't you let me come in and deejay from nine to eleven. You'll hear how I play." I'd just talk my way into it. Then I got all my friends calling up the clubs saying, "Oh, is it really true that Jellybean's deejaying there?"

> *I was always figuring out ways to make things happen.*

Once I was working, I positioned myself so that people thought, "He follows through, he's good, a nice kid, he works hard." Through my experiences of being a deejay I learned what people liked and what they didn't like about records. Then I had the opportunity to go to recording studios because the record companies and producers were bringing me records and wanting me to try them out. I would say, well, the intro isn't long enough, or this part doesn't work, and this thing's too loud, and people are not going to like this. And then they'd go back to the studio and change it.

I started saying, "If I play this and tell you what I think, what works and what doesn't work, I want you to let me come and watch you fix it. That way I can be more helpful to you when you bring it in. I'll be able to say, oh, well, change this, change that. So when I went to the studios I just wrote down everything they said—harmonizer, digital delay, reverb, echo. When they took a break I'd talk to the recording engineer. I'd say, what is reverb, what is echo? I started befriending a lot of musicians, and songwriters, and background singers, and the engineers.

Before long, everybody started saying, "Talk to Jellybean, he's a record producer." I had never produced a record in my life. But I became a production assistant. I was really good at talking my way into situations, learning about them, becoming good at them, and then using that to springboard to the next move.

One day a record producer asked me how much I would charge for doing a job for him. "You'll have to talk to my manager," I said. So I had my mom call him. "Tell him you're my manager. If he asks something you don't know just say, hold on, my other line's ringing."

When my mom called him, the guy wanted to know how much I would charge. At the time I was twenty-two years old, making $200 a night as a deejay. I said, okay, well, I'm going to be there all night, so let's charge him $400, equal to two nights of deejaying. That's a good price. So my mom tells the guy, "Four hundred," and he agreed. I thought, "Oh, no, I should've asked for more!"

So I did it for $400, but the most important thing to me was to get my name on that label and then to get test pressings, which are the versions of the records before they come out. That was very exciting. After a while I had produced a bunch of small street records that were gold singles here in New York. They mostly came from the underground.

Then I was asked to do "Flashdance" for Irene Cara, and that was when I thought, "I'm out of here now with this one because this is a movie!" Giorgio Moroder produced it. He had done Donna Summer, and he was my idol as a producer. Then I did "Maniac," then in the same week I was asked to do "Say Say Say" by Paul McCartney and Michael Jackson, "Love Is a Battlefield" by Pat Benatar, and "Tell Her About It" by Billy Joel.

I had been approached by Madonna to remix some songs for her first album, including "Lucky Star." When I was mixing the whole album they needed one more song and I had a demo from one of the singers I had met at the studio. It was a song called "Holiday." Madonna needed a song, so I figured, "Here's my opportunity!" I played it for her and she loved it. I said, "If you love the song, I'm the person that's going to fix it and make it work. Just think about it. You'll be the first record company to hire a club deejay to produce a club artist. How credible can that be?" So they said, "Great, go and do it."

I gave out the record to all the radio stations in New York, all my deejay friends. I had them all playing the record. By the time the album was released, everybody was playing "Holiday," which took off and became a number one dance record and a top ten pop hit. And then they released "Borderline," which was another song I did.

I've heard all kinds of horror stories in the music business, people getting ripped off and taken advantage of. But even with the first couple of records I did that went on to sell millions of dollars and made people millionaires, even though I walked away with only a thousand dollars at the time, I felt I was properly rewarded because I used that opportunity to get to the next one. And there are people around me who made millions ten years ago who are broke today. They didn't plan for the future.

> *I treat every penny I make like it is my last one. And I live every day of my life like it's my last one.*

My greatest day was when Madonna's "Crazy for You," which I produced, went to number one. It was the first song of mine that went to number one on the pop chart. No one thought anything could replace "We Are the World." It had been up there for nine weeks. My song came out and was at number two when "We Are the World" came out and passed it. For six or seven weeks it was number one and I was number two. But then the "We Are the World" thing finally died and my record went to number one. That was a good day.

I've always had this unquenchable thirst for knowledge.

But I have an unorthodox way of acquiring it. I figure out things backwards. I'm a self-taught musician, I'm a self-taught recording engineer, I'm a self-taught businessman.

In twelve years I've had over thirty number one records and over ninety top ten hits in America. I've probably sold a billion records worldwide. I have three films coming out this year and my company has sixteen records on the chart this week. I've had my share of failures, too. But if you fear failure you can never be successful.

Sure, I have fear, but I always come back to, well, if I don't try it I won't know. What's the worst thing that can happen? I'll fail, but if I fail then I'll know. I never wanted to live my life saying, "I could have, I would have, I should have, if only." Life's too short!

Jellybean Benitez is Chairman and CEO of Jellybean Productions, Inc. of New York City, a multimedia company with divisions in music publishing, record, film, and television production. He grew up in a Puerto Rican family in the South Bronx, attended Baruch College and the New School for Social Research, and began working as a club dee-jay at seventeen, becoming a record producer several years later. He has produced records that have sold 1 billion copies worldwide, for artists including Madonna, Whitney Houston, Billy Joel, and Michael Jackson.

Whether you're the first Latino President of the United States or an assembly-line worker, never be afraid to admit your mistakes.

Jorge Diaz
Vice President and Deputy Program Manager
Northrop Grumman Corp. B-2 Division

I was the chief engineer for the maiden flight of the B-2 "Stealth" Bomber on July 15, 1989. The B-2 is a huge long-range bomber originally designed for nuclear weapons, now a conventional bomber. It's a two-man crew, totally computerized plane, a beautiful flying machine. It has tremendous capabilities for the protection of our country.

On the day of the first scheduled flight, we had two thousand guests there—congressmen, military brass, workers, management, the press, live TV, you name it. I was in the control room and we were having problems. My bosses were standing behind me. It was a warm day and our fuel was overheating on the ground. I started getting very uneasy. I stood up in the control room and stopped everything. "We're aborting the flight, we're not flying today." I said point-blank, "We do not know what we're doing at this point. So we won't fly today."

Then I just walked out of the room. The success or failure of that flight was my job and my responsibility. I had to be accountable. If it had failed, human lives could have been lost and the costs at stake were in the hundreds of millions of dollars.

During the weekend we did a lot of testing on the aircraft, and pretty soon we found out what was wrong, we corrected it, and we flew on Monday, July 17. A very successful flight. If we'd flown the first time, there was a chance that the fuel system would have cut off during the flight, and the plane would have had to glide to an emergency landing.

You always protect the crew first, the aircraft, and the mission, in that order of priority. And when in doubt you have to be conservative. After the flight, my boss came and thanked me for aborting that first flight. "I didn't understand it then," he said, "but I do now."

We all make mistakes. But if you try to hide them, or shade them, that's the worst lack of professional integrity you can have. And it always catches up with you.

The best thing you can do is be candid, declare you made a mistake, then do your utmost to correct it. Whatever your job and your responsibility is, you're always accountable for the failures as well as the successes.

═══════════════════

You've got to stand for something, or you'll fall for anything.

Angel Martinez
President and CEO
The Rockport Company

I joined Reebok in 1980. I was the fourth employee.

I was familiar with Reebok as a product because I'd worn their shoes in high school running track. A friend of mine was considering whether to be a sales rep for the company. I knew a lot about running shoes then and a lot about running shoe companies. "You'd better be careful," I told her. "This is probably not going to fly. The running shoe market is pretty saturated. There is a whole rash of competitors out there. To start up a running shoe company at this point is a little late in the game. Some of these guys have a lot of money behind them."

We both went to a trade show in Chicago, and that's where I met Reebok's CEO, Paul Fireman, who at the time was pretty overweight. His head of sales was a guy who was a chain-smoker. Here are these two guys, one's real heavy and the other's a chain smoker, and they're trying to sell running shoes to distance runners. "What's wrong with this picture?" I asked myself. "You guys may have a great product," I told them, "but I'll never buy it from you. I don't see how you could possibly have any credibility selling running shoes to runners."

Their response to that was: "Well, if you know so much, why don't you show us how to do it?" So I started working the booth and I sold a bunch of shoes. I joined the company in 1980 as a sales rep. But in 1981 the running shoe market started to plateau. The boom was waning. If your company wasn't already up in a certain tier, you weren't going to make it. And Reebok had a very small niche of the market.

Both the low point and the high point occurred simultaneously. Driving back from a money-losing three-week trip to Oregon and Washington, I figured, "I've got to do something here. This is not good." Somewhere south of Seattle, it hit me that we needed something different to sell. Why didn't we start selling shoes for something new and popular I had observed in my region called aerobics?

Let's do an aerobic shoe. And I knew exactly what the shoe should look like. I wanted the fit and feel of a jazz dance shoe, because that's what a lot of women were wearing, with the cushion of a running shoe and the stability of a court shoe. I had the shoe designed in my head before I even got home.

I called Paul Fireman at home and said, "Paul, we've got to do aerobics."

He said, "What's aerobics?"

I explained it to him and said I wanted to design a shoe for aerobics and sell them to aerobics instructors at a special price because if aerobics instructors bought them, then every one of their students would buy them. "What we need to make is a very feminine, very comfortable, very appropriate shoe for aerobics," I said, "and I think I have the shoe in mind."

He didn't approve the idea.

I was in cahoots with the guy who was head of manufacturing for us and I got him to make me a sample shoe, just as I had sketched it. He elaborated on it and improved it. Then I went around and showed it to all these aerobics instructors and they said, "That's it. We love it. When can we get it?" So I took orders from them, then I called Paul and said, "Listen, I've got about three hundred orders here."

"Well, you can't do that," he said. "You can't sell to aerobics instructors because our retailers will get mad." So I said, "What retailers? We're not going to have any retailers here in about a month."

He told me not to do it. But I just did it anyway. I took the orders, then got the head of manufacturing to make a run of the product. I had them shipped to my house and I sent them out to the instructors. Reebok was financing it, but Paul didn't know we were doing this.

About a month later I had about a thousand orders, because the instructors had been wearing the shoes and now their students wanted them. I sent Paul a box full of orders. At that point he got it. He became the champion of the project. The aerobics shoe industry was born, and the Reebok Free-style Aerobic Shoe became the best-selling shoe in history.

> *You've got to live with the consequences of your own actions. You have to be accountable.*

I was 100 percent convinced and committed to what I was doing and I was either going to do it with Paul or without him. If he had sent me a bill for all those aerobics shoes, I would have paid him. But I would have taken the idea to somebody else or started up my own shoe company. The fact is that you've got to be willing to take a stand. Paul says it best: "You've got to stand for something, or you'll fall for anything." And when he sees that in a person, he lets them go for it.

It was a dirty job meeting with all those aerobics instructors, but somebody had to do it!

If it's your mistake, it's up to you to fix it.

Dan Gomez
President
Bell Atlantic Directory Graphics

WHEN I interview people, one of the questions I always ask them is what their biggest failure was and what they learned from it. Their ability to identify clearly what their mistakes were is a good indication that they won't ever repeat them.

I've made a few mistakes in my career that I still remember. One of them was when I was in charge of quality for a division and we rolled out a series of new concepts every year, and behind the concepts we had teams organized around action plans for the company. Everything worked smoothly until one year when I made a mistake. I got too far ahead of my bosses, and they weren't ready to support some of the new concepts. So I ended up having to backtrack, get their support for what they were willing to do, and then roll out.

It was kind of embarrassing. It wasn't difficult to figure out that I had screwed up, because everybody and their mother told me! Everybody from the president on down gave me specific and clear feedback on how I had screwed up.

How did it feel? It felt terrible. But what I did was I admitted the mistake and I told them how I thought I could fix it. The lesson I learned is that you have to make sure that the things you're trying to do are consistent with what your company wants to do, and take the time to sell your ideas to the people who count.

Don't pretend you know everything. Nobody expects you to know everything.

Jose Bared
CEO, Farm Stores

YOU need to focus, but you also need to maintain a broader vision.

You have to look at the trees, but you also have to look at the forest and be aware that it's there.

I've found A students working for B students in companies owned by C students. That was a big surprise. I thought the geniuses in the class were going to be the dominant figures in the business world. It turns out that it's not necessarily so. The reason is, perhaps, the A student got too focused, and forgot about the forest and only looked at the trees. And he was not willing to take risks. A lot of very, very bright people lack the ability to communicate. They have all of this knowledge, but they can't get it across.

Stay in touch, listen, talk to people, ask questions.

There is never a stupid question. There may be redundant questions but not stupid questions. Just ask. You're not expected to know everything. It is perfectly okay to ask questions, no matter how long you've been in the business or how much experience you have. It doesn't degrade you to ask the question.

Entrepreneurs are totally confident about asking very basic questions because it's their money. Whereas oftentimes if you don't own a piece of the business, you're afraid of looking stupid. A lot of people feel they have to fit a mold. "If I'm a manager, I can't ask a junior associate for his or her opinion." Why not? And if someone asks you a question and you don't know the answer, say, "Let me study that and get back to you."

Sometimes people think they're supposed to know all the answers. One of the first things you have to recognize is to be honest and admit that you don't know all the answers.

Jose P. Bared was CEO of Bared & Company and is now CEO of Farm Stores, both companies based in Miami, Florida. Bared & Company is a mechanical and electrical engineering company with offices in Miami, Puerto Rico, Tampa, and Atlanta. In 1992, Bared bought Farm Stores, a chain of 200 convenience stores and a dairy processing plant, all located in Florida, and turned it around from bankruptcy to profitability in 60 days. He was born in Cuba and obtained an engineering degree from the University of Miami.

OFF THE RECORD

It's hard, but put some limits on your "Latino guilt"!

**39-year-old chief information officer
of a transportation company**

YOU may think, *"Oh, Dios mío,* if I make a mistake, I'm fulfilling all the misperceptions of Latinos!" But no matter how hard you try, you'll never be perfect. Forgive yourself for making mistakes and realize the enormous dangers of refusing to admit them.

Even if you graduated at the top of your class and your group is 300 percent more profitable than any other in the company, if you screw up, and, let's face it, you will, there are others in the company who will conclude that you're a "token Hispanic," a "quota," an "affirmative action baby." There's not much you can do about that.

Always remember that you and everyone else in the company are going to make mistakes at some point, and you can't beat yourself up too much because of them. Admit the mistake, don't overflagellate yourself, absorb the learning, and move on.

I learned a very important lesson: being up front with people works.

**Robert Behar
President
Hero Productions**

THE worst time in my career was when we were broken into and got wiped out. We were a small business and didn't have insurance. All of our advisors said, "Declare bankruptcy, declare bankruptcy!"

But I was of the old school that says you don't welsh on your debts. So I called in all our creditor companies and I was very up front with them. "Listen," I said. "We were broken into. We had almost $100,000 worth of stuff stolen. It's going to create a burden on us. But we're going to come back. Please work with us and we'll make sure you get paid all we owe you. And if we have to pay you some interest on the debt, we'll pay you the interest."

Of the eight companies we had credit with, seven went along with us. We paid everybody back and got ourselves back in business.

Robert Behar is President of Miami-based Hero Productions, the only full-service television production facility and international teleport in the Southeast. He was born in Cuba, attended college in Miami, and in 1978 founded Hero Communications, an international distributor of equipment for the satellite, cable, and wireless television industries.

===

Fear of failure is a great motivator. A little fear doesn't hurt.

Natica del Valle von Althann
Managing Director
Citibank

WHEN I first started working at a major bank, I was ill-prepared for the job. I felt insecure and frightened. Even though I was educated, I was standing side by side with freshly minted MBAs who also probably had work experience. So I felt at a disadvantage. I developed the worst case of Mylanta for the next two years.

Number one, you've got to try harder in a situation like that. Any group that has to break in, whether it be a BA in an MBA world, or a woman in a man's world, or a minority in a field that's not accustomed to having different people, I think the only way you earn respect is to just be better and more capable, and by using your street smarts.

I was a trainee in the Correspondent Banking Group, and my training officer was taking me through a whirlwind tour of the Midwest, visiting seventeen correspondent banks in one week. I had to prepare the information packages for all seventeen visits, attend the meetings, write the call reports and organize the follow-up. So I made sure that I was superbly organized for the task, and fear was my motivator.

> *If you're too comfortable early on in your career, you are probably in trouble. Either you're not working hard enough or you're not wide awake.*

Many people were washed out of my training program as a result of that trip. I came back and made sure that within five days all of those seventeen reports were done. First impressions are important.

> *When you're young and at the bottom of the pack, don't stand on your high horse and ask for the golden projects. Take the tough assignments and make something out of them. That's the perfect chance to show your mettle.*

Rise to the challenge. At this stage in your career, you're in no position to be a prima donna. You're in no position to demand. Why should you? They're taking a bet on you. You now have to show them that their bet was well placed. You've got to produce. So take on projects that no one has produced on before and make something out of them. I concentrated on knotty problems. For example, I had a cement company client who wanted to develop a huge dam in Brazil in conjunction with another European partner. I brought in our international finance group to put together the largest project financing ever done in Latin America. It was a highly unusual, highly distinctive deal. I introduced the idea, sold it to my client, and then let our expert group on the subject execute it. I stayed on top of it to help resolve conflicts and make sure it stayed on track.

The way to succeed is to go after the difficult value-added situations. Don't compete for a me-too position. Identify a special problem that needs handling and come up with a unique solution.

I turned down prestigious assignments for what were considered the dregs, but which I felt would teach me skills. Was that the right move for me? Definitely.

Skill building in different key areas is an important part of any early career path. Seek opportunities that build upon or expand your present skill base. Don't go for the key or glamour jobs early on.

Panic can be a healthy thing.

Oscar de la Renta
Founder, Chairman, and CEO
Oscar de la Renta, Inc.

BUSINESS is a risk on practically a daily basis. For example, my first show in Europe several years ago was a very calculated risk. No American designer had ever put on a fashion show in Paris before. And if the collection wasn't good and the show was a big flop, the whole thing would probably backfire. But I had been designing clothes for over twenty-five years and I knew I could take the risk.

This is a business with tremendous built-in insecurity, because you're only as good as your last collection. So there was the obvious risk that I might have a collection that bombed, and they would say, "What a mistake to come to Paris." Well, I could have bombed in New York as well. As it turned out, the show was a huge success.

> *In any creative work there is a great deal of insecurity, but that self-doubt is what moves you on to really try to prove to yourself that you can do it.*

There is one time in my work which I call "panic time." It's the last twenty days before a show when I really feel panic. I go to bed and can barely sleep. But then eventually I see light at the end of the tunnel and I start to feel a little more sure about what I'm doing. Then there are other times when you feel you can do anything, because your energy is flowing and everything is going full speed.

The fashion designer Bill Blass and I are very close friends. He told me that many people say he must have it easier now, since after so many years it has to be a cinch to design a collection. But he and I agreed that actually we get more and more panicked as we grow older, because there are so many young people coming along and you feel the pressure of all the competition. At the same time, because you are demanding of yourself as a professional, you feel that each time you have to do better.

I don't expect it ever to get any easier.

> *You can only be creative and succeed in business when you have a passion for what you are doing and a passion for that business.*

If you are really ambitious and you want to be successful, there is agony on a daily basis, but at the same time there is tremendous pleasure. It's the pleasure of succeeding, of doing well. There's no great mystery to success. It's just a lot of work!

Oscar de la Renta is Founder, Chairman, and CEO of Oscar de la Renta, Inc. of New York City, a global fashion, cosmetics, and fragrance company with sales estimated by industry sources at $500 million. He was born in Santo Domingo, the Dominican Republic, began his career as an apprentice fashion designer in Europe, and came to the United States in 1962 to build de la Renta into one of the most prestigious brand names in business. In 1993 he made industry history by becoming the first American designer to exhibit his collection at the Paris fashion shows. He is now opening new Oscar de la Renta boutiques in the United States, Hong Kong, Japan, Jakarta, and London, with additional openings under way.

Don't be afraid to follow your heart.

Felipe Rodriguez
President
Globo International

EARLY in my career at Pan American Airways, they gave me a briefcase and said, "You're going to be a salesman." They gave me a list of customers to call on. I went to see the first customer and I spent almost two hours frozen on the sidewalk, because I didn't have the courage to go upstairs and talk to him. I was a country boy. But after I overcame that situation, I realized that I enjoyed communications, and I was able to communicate. The first customer was from the Dominican Republic. Suddenly we started talking about culture and our love of geography. Here I was in Venezuela, a Cuban talking to a Dominican. He became one of my best customers.

I always said, "I'm going to make it." I thought that I was as capable as anybody else. I have access to all the books that other people had, I'm an avid reader. I know the world from Australia to Taiwan to Europe and Morocco. Knowledge doesn't necessarily come from a Harvard or Yale or Stanford degree. Knowledge comes from within and from what you put into yourself. I realized that perhaps I didn't have the same cultural access that I would have had at Harvard or Oxford, but I tried to compensate by reading and studying what a student at Harvard would read. I'd rather be an A plus at the University of Caracas with a lot of reading than a C minus at Harvard.

When I was vice president of Pan American, my boss was executive vice president and he was promoted to president. I knew that if I had stayed in Pan Am another year, I could have been an executive vice president. An executive from Globo approached me and said, "We want to open up an office in New York. Do you know of anybody who is bilingual?" I looked at the guy and I went into my "mental Internet," started looking into some names, and the name that came out was Felipe Rodriguez.

He looked at me as if I landed from the moon. Here I am a top executive of Pan American with a staff and secretaries and everything else, and I'm proposing myself to start a business that could not have more than six or seven employees. But I knew that something was telling me that there are times to change, there are times that you have to, as we say in Spanish, *"Renovarse es vivir"*—to renew yourself is to start a new life. I knew I might be falling into a routine, which is very common with executives in middle age. I said, no way, I need more challenges. And I have been with the Globo group now twenty-one years.

One of the best times to change industries or careers is when you are at the top. The worst thing that can happen is when they kick you out begging and screaming. Jump when you are a winner.

Felipe Rodriguez is President of Globo International (NY) LTD in New York City. He studied business and law, and has lived in Puerto Rico, Brazil, Cuba, Venezuela, Florida, and New York. He joined Pan American Airways as a cargo manager and rose to become the first Latino vice president of a major airline. He joined Globo in 1974.

There are unknowns, and there are unknown un-knowns. Know what they are.

Fernando Niebla
Founder and CEO
Infotec Development Inc.

In 1965 I went to Cape Kennedy and I was there for five years, most of the time as the supervisor for North American Rockwell in charge of a team of about 120 engineers and technicians working on the Saturn rockets, launching them to the moon. Then I moved to California to continue working for NAR. At the end of 1978, I resigned and started working full time at Infotec, a company I founded.

I mortgaged my house to start the company. I put aside some money to support my family for two years, and a part of the money went into setting up the business. I told my wife, "I don't know if this will succeed in two years. We may be back to ground zero." Her response was, "We've had a good life working with you as an engineer. So you can always go back to that."

My idea at the time was to have a consulting firm of about fifty people, so we all got together and built a very solid technical and management team. We decided we could get to $50 million, so we then proceeded to plan how we would do that, including how we would finance the company, and how we would organize to take each successive step. We actually got to $53 million. Good planning—that's basically what got the company to its present range.

The best moment was when we won our first significant contract. That was about year three in the company. The worst moments were when some of those contracts came to an end and we had to lay off people. That's always the hard part of the business.

There are a lot of unknowns when you start up a business and you have to have well-defined plans along each step of the way. You need a well-documented plan that shows that you've thought through all the problems, that you know what your unknowns are and have a way of dealing with them.

J. Fernando Niebla is Founder and CEO of Infotec Development Inc. in Santa Ana, CA. He was born in Nogales, Mexico, earned a bachelor's degree in electrical engineering at the University of Arizona, a master's degree in business administration from the University of Southern California Business School, and started his career with North American Rockwell. From 1965 to 1970 he worked at Cape Kennedy on the Saturn moon rocket. Later, he worked on satellite and space station design for NAR in California. In 1979 he started Infotec.

The worst thing would be to get to sixty-five or seventy, look back and say, "I wonder who I'd been if . . ."

> **Phil Roman**
> **Chairman and CEO**
> **Film Roman**

I'VE had a couple of disappointments. They're inevitable.

I was working as an animator at a place that was cutting back when I was offered a job somewhere else. So I told my boss and he said, "No, no, no, don't take it. You're not going to be one of the ones laid off." So I turned the job down. Then a couple of weeks later I got laid off.

I was out of work for about seven months. There were very few jobs. The whole animation industry was adjusting from the movies to television, but there weren't enough TV shows yet to employ many animators like me. So I had to reflect and say to myself, "Is this really what I want to do? I know what I want to do, but okay, what else would I want to do if I had to change?"

At one point during that period, I saw an ad in the *Los Angeles Times* from a stock brokerage firm that was looking for trainees. So I went there and applied. I did that for a few months and already had my license when Warner's called me in to work on *The Incredible Mr. Limpet*. So I was back in animation where I really wanted to be, and in 1984 I founded my own company. It's never too late—I was fifty-three years old when I started my studio.

Right now we're going through a tremendous period of growth. We don't have the money that Disney has, we don't have the money that all the major studios that we compete with have. They have very deep pockets. But we have as much capability with the TV networks and we probably have more shows on the air than most of the other studios do.

Right now we're at the stage where we're talking to investment bankers, trying to get investors in the company so we can have greater financial footing. So here I am, a right-brain kind of a guy, stuck in a room with all these left-brain people. What the hell are they talking about? All of a sudden my left brain is starting to wake up and say, hey, what's going on here? I'm having to do a lot of learning about the financial and legal aspects of my business.

We've gone from a little company that in the first year had revenues a bit under $300,000. This year it might be around $35 million. In ten years—that's fairly significant. Things like that impress the bankers. They know this business is growing, that this company is growing.

Okay, so what if I fail? I can always get a job as an animator. I can animate. I know people in the business, so I can always go out and get a job. But at least inside I'll know that I tried.

═══════════════════════

I've seen too many people too cautious, not wanting to make a mistake. They can't make a decision, they're indecisive.

Henry Gonzalez
Senior Vice President/Zone Manager
McDonald's Corporation

I joined McDonald's in 1973, starting as a manager trainee at the restaurant in my neighborhood. My father was very excited when I joined the company. He was a die-hard McDonald's customer. He somehow intuitively knew that McDonald's was a very good company. "They sell food, everybody eats, you get cash," he said. "This is a good company!" He became my most loyal customer!

McDonald's encourages its people to act as if they're owners of the company. That makes for faster decisions, running the business as if it were your own.

> *Sometimes you can get too focused on trying to be perfect, or worse, trying not to make a mistake. Making eight out of ten right decisions is a lot better than only making one decision, whether it's right or wrong.*

One time I launched a program to improve our signage to get more visibility for our restaurants. But I made the mistake of not investigating the whole scope of rules, regulations, zoning, etc. I quickly had to write off the money we invested because the signs didn't meet certain zoning requirements.

I worked my way through these first minor problems by being really persistent about it, figuring out what kind of signs we could install where they would get the greatest visibility. I just did some fundamental things that would seem obvious after the fact.

Reexamine the obvious, and understand that sometimes the solution is so fundamental that it becomes a matter of focus, persistence, not overthinking, and not trying to make the problem more complicated than it needs to be.

Henry Gonzalez is Senior Vice President/Zone Manager for McDonald's Corporation in Oak Brook, Illinois. He joined McDonald's as a trainee store manager at his local restaurant in 1973 and worked his way up from area supervisor, field consultant, field service manager, training director, vice president, and corporate vice president to be appointed to his current position in 1995.

I was blessed with a lazy boss.

Linda Alvarado
President
Alvarado Construction, Inc.

PEOPLE ask me, "How did you get involved in construction?" My answer: pure unemployment. Unemployment was the best thing that ever happened to me.

Not all great careers are planned. You may get your degree in something and find out you don't like it, or you may have to settle for any job you can get. I went to college in

California but I couldn't find a job. My major was in economics. My first job was in the Botanical Gardens. A dream job. I could wear shorts to work, get a tan. But I ended up overwatering the plants and killing them, so it was clear that a career in landscaping was not for me.

I finally got another job with a developer, and when the company started a construction management group, I was transferred into it. I had a boss I owe a lot to. In a way he was not an intentional mentor, he was an accidental mentor. At the time I thought he was extraordinarily lazy. He loved to play golf. He had an affinity for long lunches. So he was very skillful at delegating his responsibilities. But what really enabled me to establish a niche was the fact that computerized scheduling programs had just begun to come on-line, and my boss let me develop an expertise in this area.

For years, construction people used to meet for coffee and schedule the day's work on the back of a napkin. When I learned computerized scheduling, I acquired a skill that many men did not yet have. And this specialty niche allowed me to develop invaluable expertise in the industry.

My approach to life is do the best you can with what's in front of you. Worry as little as possible or maybe not at all about things that are not within your control.

Eduardo Aguirre
Senior Vice President
and Division Executive
NationsBank

IF you have confidence in yourself, in the long run things will work out. That's one of the blessings we have in this country—you can really rise above all kinds of circumstances. Except on rare occasions, you can overcome all sorts of difficulties. Just because you don't do well at school or work in a particular year, that should not prevent you from sticking to it and charging forward.

I've been with NationsBank now for eighteen years or so. At one point the bank got into serious trouble in Texas because of bad energy and real estate loans. People were being laid off and fired right and left and my job was as vulnerable as anybody else's could've been.

Then my boss asked me do a study which analyzed international private banking in a conglomeration of banks that was merging into this bank. I did the study and found international private banking to be a substantial line of business. I reported that to my boss and he said, "Okay, we want you to head that business for us in the new organization."

"Absolutely not," I said. "I don't want to do this. It's just not in my makeup. This is more of a retail type of organization, and I'm more of a wholesale banker. I'm more of a corporate banker. I just don't want to do it."

"You really don't understand," my boss said. "This is not a suggestion. This is your job or you're on your way."

"Well," I said, "I see what you mean."

I went home very despondent, thinking I had been handed a very poor opportunity. I could not have been more wrong.

> *I did not have a choice at that point, and I chose to turn that circumstance into an opportunity.*

One thing led to another and all of a sudden I'm heading an organization that has about eighty people and is managing about $2.5 billion in assets. The lesson I learned is to accept challenges and try to make the best of what might seem to be bad situations.

If you're so sensitive to criticism that you don't hear it, you can really be doomed.

Nely Galan
President, Galan Entertainment
20th Century Fox

ONE of the biggest lessons I've learned is to never be defensive and to take criticism well. When people criticize me or say to me, "I think you're screwing up," I listen. And I really take it in.

Sometimes I think the person's wrong. But I try to really integrate the criticism into my life. I don't see it as if somebody's hurting me. I try to be objective. I like myself, I don't have a problem with that. But if somebody thinks that I can improve somehow, I react to that criticism in a way that will be most useful to me.

When I tell somebody on my staff, "This is where you could be doing better" and they get defensive, it really makes me want to scream. I think criticism is your friend— as painful as it may be.

You can learn a lot from rejection.

Linda Alvarado
President
Alvarado Construction, Inc.

IF my construction company doesn't get a particular project, I ask for a debriefing to try to figure out what went wrong. Debriefings are a tradition in my business. And I have found that there are people within any organization who will open that door. You just have to find that person,

that one believer. He may say, "This project is too important, the schedule is too critical, the budget's too tight, we
can't afford to go with a smaller firm or an entry-level firm.
We need XYZ company that's big and has been in business
for fifty years. They've done it before, they can do it again.
It's not broke, why fix it?" Rather than giving up, asking for
that kind of feedback can be very helpful in preparing for
the next proposal or the next job or the next interview.

I found that men are more comfortable with men, and
when I first started doing business I used to sign with my
initials so they wouldn't know if Alvarado was a man or a
woman. It was a very thin disguise, but it did not raise a
question about my company's ability. But you learn from
debriefings and rejections. Your perception of why you
didn't get a certain job may not be correct. In some cases I
thought I was the problem. But they said, no, your price
was wrong. Today I sign our proposals with my full name.

It's not pleasant to sit down and find out what you did
wrong. On the other hand, very often you find that people
will volunteer information that otherwise you couldn't get.
You also create relationships. People start getting to know
what you're all about. And in telling you why you weren't
chosen, you get to know what they are all about. So next
time, you'll be able to go in and say, We really understand
your situation. We really want to do work for you.

Some people give up after just one rejection, rather than
going back repeatedly and finally getting it right. So don't
assume that a rejection is permanent. Or that you'll never
do business with that company. That might be the case, but
you have no way of testing it unless you ask why you were
rejected.

INSIGHT 6

═══════════════

ORGULLO
(PRIDE)

Be proud of who you are, be proud of your culture and language. You will do well and you will mix beautifully in both cultures.

I was American way before you were!

Oscar de la Renta
Founder, Chairman, and CEO
Oscar de la Renta, Inc.

SOMETIMES people hear my accent and ask me, "Are you American?"

I say, "Yes."

And they say, "Where do you come from?"

"I come from the Dominican Republic."

They say, "Oh, but then you're not American."

I say, "Yes, actually, my island was the very first island in the New World. Every one of the early expeditions started from Santo Domingo."

I joke about it, but I am very proud of my heritage. I always say, "I was American way before you were!"

Hispanics can be the inspiration to all America because we still see this country as the incredible opportunity that it really is.

Angel Martinez
President and CEO
The Rockport Company

YOU have a lot of people saying so many negative things about America, but the fact is it's the best country in the world, and that's why so many people, especially from Latin America, come here. That can be lost on people who have grown up here.

> *This is still the land of opportunity, if you're from El Salvador, Guatemala, Mexico, Cuba, it doesn't matter. Hispanic cultural traits like family and hard work are crucial competitive assets for this country into the next millennium.*

I really want people who have my background to understand the unique role they have to play in where this country is going and not to abdicate it. If you sit back and say, "Hand it over to me, or give it to me because I deserve it," then you deserve what you get. And in the end we're all going to be far worse off.

I've seen bigotry. But I always take it as a challenge. I have to rise above it and show that I'm a hell of a lot more than what their small minds might lead them to believe. But I don't stand for bigotry, obviously. I don't put up with it. I choose my friends pretty carefully. People who don't want to deal with me because I'm Hispanic, frankly, I feel they're the ones who are losing out. I don't lose any sleep over it.

I was born in the Andes mountains and I see every challenge as a mountain.

Lucia DeGarcia
President and CEO
Élan International

I know that behind each mountain there's always another one you have to overcome. But you have to create your own opportunities.

If you believe in yourself and you believe you can do something, you will make it happen because this is a country of opportunities. If you can't do it here you can't do it anywhere.

In order to succeed, we must be proud of our cul-ture, of our language, and of ourselves. We must believe that we are as good as anyone else. When we believe it, we will be comfortable with our-selves and able to mix beautifully in both the Latino culture and the American culture.

Lionel Sosa
Chairman
DMB&B/Américas
Founder, Sosa, Bromley, Aguilar, Noble & Associates

I was born on the west side of San Antonio—the Hispanic side of town. My parents taught my two brothers, my sister, and me to have pride in our culture and in our language. I remember Mom saying, "Lionel, you will be able to accom-plish anything you want, even though you're Mexican." I didn't realize then what a mixed message she was sending. Half of it was positive and the other half was negative.

She was right. I did accomplish everything I wanted in life, but underneath, I always had the feeling that I was not "equal." So I worked harder than anyone. I made a special effort to be "as good as the Anglo."

My parents also taught us to *understand* the Anglo. "When you grow up, you're going to be doing business with the Anglo," they said. "That's where the money is. So make sure you understand them, make sure you do what they want." That lesson has served me well as I move around the Anglo corporate world today.

As a youngster, I was educated in public schools with almost 100 percent Latino kids. Sadly, public schools in Hispanic neighborhoods at the time were really trade schools, not college preparatory schools. They taught us to be good with our hands: to upholster cars, to repair them, to be carpenters and draftsmen, to be artists. The message the school administration was sending was that Latinos were not college material.

Yet, through all those mixed mesages we received, we were taught through hard work anything is possible. I began to dream about big things. My biggest dream was to work for Disney as an illustrator. I applied, but they didn't hire me. So I came back to San Antonio and used my portfolio to try to land a job in advertising.

I didn't get an offer there either. But I was offered a position as a sign designer. I took it and stayed at Texas Neon Advertising for eight years. There I learned the value of teamwork and camaraderie. Everyone helped each other. I learned to respect differences. I learned to respect similarities. I learned to get my hands dirty.

This training and these messages guided my professional career. I learned to work hard. I learned to work with corporate America, I learned the value of pride and teamwork. I also learned the importance of my culture and my language. And I made a career where I can put all of that to work, Hispanic advertising.

The agency I started grew from zero to revenues of over $100 million. Today, Sosa, Bromley, Aguilar, Noble & Associates is the largest Hispanic agency in the United States. It employs 140 professionals, mostly Hispanic, who are entrusted with handling multimillion-dollar budgets and strategic plans for Fortune 500 companies. I'm very proud of my people and of my partners, Ernest Bromley and Al Aguilar. We've accomplished a lot together.

Lionel Sosa is Chairman of DMB&B/Américas and Founder of Sosa, Bromley, Aguilar, Noble & Associates in San Antonio, Texas. He was born in San Antonio of parents who immigrated from Mexico. From age eighteen to twenty-six, he was a commercial sign designer, then opened his own graphic art studio, which he transformed into Sosa & Associates in 1981. Today, the Sosa agency is one of twenty that make up DMB&B/Américas, a network of Latin American agencies that Sosa oversees. DMB&B/Américas has billings of $500 million a year.

People ask me, "Do you ever think of changing your name?"

Antonio Rodriguez
Senior Vice President
Seagram Spirits and Wine Group

SOME people have asked me, "Do you ever have a problem because so many Puerto Ricans are running around with your name?"

"What problem?" I say. "It's a free country. I don't own the name."

Latinos who don't have a very obviously Latino last name avoid these hassles. But I would never think of changing my name. It's something that's very important to me because it's the name my father gave me. If I change my name it would be like disowning him. I know some people do that, and I'm not criticizing them for doing it. But I'm very proud of my family and heritage, so I'm willing to take the licks.

The important thing is remembering who we are, where we came from, and how we got here.

Linda Alvarado
President
Alvarado Construction, Inc.

I tell my children that we are descended from great builders, mathematicians, and scientists. Our forefathers were the architects and builders of pyramids, viaducts, cities, and highways. We were already living in very sophisticated cities on this continent. We were the aristocracy, the landowners, the merchants, the attorneys, long before the Europeans ever came to America.

There are still pockets of resistance and stereotypical notions about us, even today. But I think it's changing. If you look at the titles now associated with Hispanic surnames—governor, mayor, CEO—we are returning to positions that we once held long ago. I don't make tortillas every morning like my mother did, but the values of family, tradition, and religion have been important in our culture for centuries, and they are the things that Latinos work very, very hard to retain.

What's in a name?

Sergio Leiseca
Partner
Baker & McKenzie

My identity is very important to me. And something that really burns me is the terrible pronunciation of Latino names—they get butchered. And then if you don't correct people, you end up with a mispronounced name.

At one point in my life it would make me angry when someone mispronounced my name, almost as if I didn't belong. These days I'm a little bit more secure. If someone mispronounces my name, I simply correct him. And we go on from there.

By the same token, I don't disguise the fact that I can speak Spanish. My secretary is from Venezuela, so she and I speak Spanish most of the time. Not that I want to speak

Spanish in front of people who don't understand it, if it makes them uncomfortable. You don't have to point out differences just for the sake of pointing them out. But at the same time, you want to be yourself, and if you want to speak Spanish, you speak Spanish.

═══════════

I value my name and I value my heritage.

Solomon Trujillo
President and CEO
U S WEST Communications Group

SOME Latinos have Americanized their names. For example, if their name was Trujillo, like mine, they'd pronounce it "Tru-jello." Not our family! And even today, if people inside or outside the company mispronounce my name, I make it a point to correct them.

Sometimes I'll say, "In case you missed how I pronounce my name," and then I'll write it out for them—"Tru-HEE-yo."

It sends a signal about the importance of my name. I value my name and my heritage. I always try to take the time to make sure I know how to pronounce other people's names. And I expect the same in return. It's a matter of mutual respect.

═══════════

OFF THE RECORD

The least you can do is get the name right.

40-year-old consumer products
marketing executive

I was interviewing someone for a job with my company. She was Latina but she understood that just because I had a

Spanish last name, as she did, I wasn't going to give her any special consideration. She didn't say, "Hey, we're both Latinos." She was very professional. And that's why I was surprised when I got her courtesy thank-you note after the interview. She got my name wrong. I have a common Latino name and she had addressed me by another common Latino name. My colleagues couldn't believe it!

The mistake she made was something many non-Latinos do often—"Gomez, Lopez, Fernandez, your names all sound alike." But she of all people should not have made that same mistake.

Was I offended? No. I laughed it off, but the laugh was really on her. I mean if you're willing to overlook that kind of basic thing I can't trust you. I wasn't being prejudiced against her, I was saying, "This is dumb."

You should hold yourself to the same standard regardless of where you come from. Don't make those kinds of mistakes.

═══════════════════════════

What you can't do is lose your identity—who you are and what matters to you.

Lydia Hernández-Vélez
Senior Vice President
CoreStates Financial

I grew up and went to high school in the South Bronx during a period of "transition." We were the second Puerto Rican family on the block. During my high school years the major shift came—the whites went to Co-op City in the North Bronx, and the school became predominantly black and Latino.

I tell people I lived in a piece of Puerto Rico that landed in New York, because all my parents' friends and everybody who socialized with them were from a few towns in Puerto Rico. I count myself very lucky to come from a really strong family. My mother battled with the school all the way from kindergarten: "My daughter isn't learning in this class, you have to move her." She wouldn't stop until they moved me. She was just like my great-grandmother, who was a very tough cookie—she was a legend in her hometown.

Sometimes we forget that our parents faced some incredible obstacles—for example, it wasn't always politically incorrect to call you a "spic." Even today, it's terribly frustrating for me when I watch television and they portray Puerto Rico as if it were nothing but mud huts. We can't let Puerto Ricans and Latinos be defined by the media.

When I took the subway into Manhattan to attend Barnard College, it seemed like a different world, and I had to negotiate my way through it. The tough part was feeling like I was drowning, and I didn't know how deep deep was! I just knew I had to rely on myself and my family.

There were times when I worked in Legal Services, and someone would question my judgment because of my name or who they thought I was. How did I deal with it? I did my homework. I proved myself with my performance.

One of my best days was when I went to work here at CoreStates. This bank has given me some very interesting jobs, which years ago I probably wouldn't have been considered for, simply because of my background. The management of this bank has said, "We will foreclose no one from providing a value to the corporation."

Develop a thick skin. Never forget that no one manages your career but you. Abdicate that to no one. You are your own corporation. You "lease yourself" to your company. I lease myself to this company—my talents, my intelligence, and everything I bring to it. Nobody is accountable or responsible for my success but me. If I make the sacrifice and get up at four in the morning to read something I think will help me, it's worth it.

Lydia Hernández-Vélez is Senior Vice President of CoreStates Financial Corporation in Philadelphia. She grew up in the South Bronx, earned a bachelor of arts degree from Barnard College, a law degree from Hofstra University, and began her career as a Community Legal Services attorney. She joined CoreStates in 1990, and currently manages the bank's Legal and Corporate Compliance departments.

═══════════════

I have always been tremendously competitive— never satisfied with anything less than winning.

Arturo J. González
Partner
Morrison & Foerster

My father immigrated to this country from Mexico in 1955. He brought my mother and their five children to California in 1959. I was born the following year. I spent many years as a child working in the fields throughout northern California. Most of our summers were spent picking peaches, although we also picked tomatoes and plums. I can still recall being forced to wake up at 4:30 A.M. and being served *chocolate* (hot chocolate) for breakfast. By 5:00 A.M., my two older brothers, my mother, my younger sister, and I were driving to the fields. I worked in the fields until I was in the sixth grade.

My parents do not have any formal education. My father worked for the Southern Pacific railroad. He was on a traveling work crew. He would leave on Sunday afternoon and not return until Friday afternoon. Although we did not spend much time together, I always respected my father because he was hard-working.

Given my background, you might expect that I would end up in a low-paying job, on welfare, in prison, or worse. For reasons I cannot fully understand, I was luckier than that. Ever since I can remember, I have always been interested in school and in learning.

The most significant motivating factor in my life was the

injustice that I perceived as a child and as a young man. I still recall the confusion when the immigration trucks came screeching in to arrest people who were working in the fields. Many of the workers ran; some managed to escape. I never understood why so many families were taken away. Even worse, both of my older brothers had unfortunate encounters with the police. Long before the Rodney King video and Mark Fuhrman tapes, these experiences led me to believe that to protect my family and my people, I had to master the law.

No one in my family had attended college. Fortunately, my sister Eva helped me to complete the necessary paperwork, and I was admitted to the University of California at Davis.

Although my high school grades were good, I did not complete the requisite courses for college admission. U.C. Davis nonetheless gave me the opportunity to enroll through its Educational Opportunity Program, otherwise known as affirmative action.

When I entered U.C. Davis, I knew that I wanted to be a lawyer. Prior to my freshman year, I painted "Harvard or Bust" on my 1965 Volkswagen Beetle. I graduated, with honors, in 1982, with a bachelor's degree in political science-public service, and then went off to Harvard.

Moving to Cambridge, Massachusetts was difficult. I had never been on an airplane. Outside of a few trips to visit family in Los Angeles and the Bay Area, I had never been more than 50 miles from my parents' home. I knew very little about what to expect in law school, and I knew nothing about the east coast. As silly as it may seem, I spent a considerable amount of time worrying about whether I would have adequate supplies. I felt as though I was traveling to another planet.

I graduated from law school in June 1985 and began working full-time at Morrison & Foerster that fall. I chose Morrison & Foerster because of the firm's commitment to providing legal services to the poor. I joined the litigation department in San Francisco. Although I was only twenty-five, my starting salary was nearly double what my father had earned the previous year (after nearly thirty years with the railroad). A few months after I began working, my father retired. I went to work with my father on his last day. What I recall most about that day is that after nearly twenty-nine years of service, my father was not allowed to go home early on his last day of work. Characteristically, he did not complain.

The legal profession has changed significantly in the past ten years. In 1985, there was so much legal work that law firms could not hire enough lawyers. Today, the legal market has shifted dramatically. More of our clients are doing their own legal work in-house, and many others are demanding the same quality work product, but at a lower cost. Law firms down-sized, and many lawyers are now looking for work. Law students graduating from the top schools still manage to land jobs with top firms, but students from many law schools are unable to find jobs.

Every student who is contemplating working at a large law firm should recognize that one of the primary factors in determining whether a young lawyer succeeds is that lawyer's ability to generate business. This is not easy for young lawyers to do, especially lawyers of color. Most of us do not have wealthy friends who can afford our high rates. For this and other reasons, there are very few minority lawyers at large law firms. When I began at Morrison & Foerster, I was the only Latino attorney in the firm. Today, of the 500 attorneys in our firm, eight are Latino.

In 1992, I became the first Latino partner at Morrison & Foerster. I have been successful in large part due to the firm's willingness to allow me to perform legal services on behalf of the poor. In 1991, the Richmond Unified School District (located in the Bay Area) announced that schools would be closing six weeks early because the District had run out of funds. With the assistance of my co-counsel

Michael Harris, I was able to obtain a preliminary injunction requiring the State of California to keep the schools open. Ultimately, Michael and I argued the case before the California Supreme Court. We won.

Working at a large law firm has allowed me to serve Latinos in a variety of cases. For example, in 1992, four Latina women were arrested at a school board meeting, subjected to a demeaning visual body cavity strip search, and charged with a variety of crimes. During the strip search, the women were forced to remove all of their clothes, and, while naked, shake their hair, squat and cough, then turn around and bend over so a deputy could inspect their body cavities. Although the ladies could not afford legal counsel, I successfully defended them in the criminal case. Following that trial, we filed a civil rights lawsuit in federal court, claiming that the strip searches violated the Fourth Amendment. A federal jury agreed, and awarded our clients $1.45 million.

> *To date, I have won all of my jury trials. The key to my success has been thorough preparation, always anticipating what move opposing attorneys might make.*

My advice to future lawyers is to work hard, be thorough, honest, and exercise good judgment. Being a lawyer is stressful and demanding, but the results achieved can be very satisfying. Remember, no matter how articulate a person might be, only lawyers are allowed to walk into a courtroom and speak on behalf of others. It is a tremendous responsibility.

Arturo J. González is a Partner of Morrison & Foerster, an international law firm headquartered in San Francisco. He was raised in

Roseville, California, a small railroad town near Sacramento. He earned a bachelor's degree in political science at the University of California at Davis, and a law degree from Harvard University.

======

The Latino experience is going to be very different for some of us than for others.

Sabino Rodriguez III
Partner
Day, Berry & Howard

I think one's Latino experience is going to depend on how "Anglo" your name is and what you look like. In my case, you can't tell me from John Smith down the hall because I don't "look Latino." So I don't think I've suffered the same kinds of prejudice that others might have suffered because of the way they look. I've had my share of trouble, though, having to deal with a name like Sabino Rodriguez.

My first year in law school, one of my professors called on me and said, "Mr. Gonzalez, what do you think about this?" I sat there, looked at him, and didn't answer. I don't really think he meant anything terrible. He just didn't care. I was going to tell him, "That's okay, all Anglo-Saxon names sound alike to me, too."

It was important not to show how demeaned it made me feel. It doesn't really help the situation.

Sabino Rodriguez III is a Partner at Day, Berry & Howard, a major law firm, and is based in their Stamford, Connecticut, office specializing in business transactions, executive compensation, and federal and state taxation. A second-generation American, he was born in Yonkers, New York, with grandparents from Colombia and Spain, and has family in Mexico, Puerto Rico, and Cuba. He obtained a bachelor's degree in government and economics and a law degree, both from Harvard University. He began his career as an attorney at Sullivan & Cromwell in New York City.

It all comes down to the things your mom and dad taught you: familia *is first, then belief in yourself and doing good in the community. These are core values.*

Frank Alvarez
Vice President
Kaiser Foundation

I was born and raised in East L.A. I came from a blue-collar family. Dad was a truck driver and Mom was a seamstress. After high school I chose public health as a career because I didn't like the way my people had been treated by the hospitals in the barrio.

We had some real small hospitals that would come and go in the span of a decade, they'd be opened and closed two or three times. When the ambulances picked us up and took our *gente* there, you'd want to get them out as fast as you could because they had reputations of being marginal in terms of quality. Oh, my God, it was total fear. We were treated like second-class citizens. So I figured I'd try to change the system from the inside out.

When I got out of college, I was accepted at Notre Dame and the University of California at Berkeley to do graduate work. My wife was pregnant at the time. We put both letters of acceptance on the table. We were living in a little *casita* in East L.A. I was working two jobs to make ends meet. I said, "Which school should I take?" My wife asked a profound question: "Does it snow in Berkeley? It snows in South Bend. So you'd better go to Berkeley because we don't have warm clothes for the kids."

I'd always lived in a community that was primarily *raza*. I was very comfortable with the group I ran with. The guys would get together on weekends and play basketball and drink beer afterward. Family would come together for all the holidays and there'd be big parties. I dressed in a certain sort of style, and wore my hair a certain way. When we moved to Berkeley for graduate school, the first thing I realized was that I was dressing funny. The leather jackets I was comfortable wearing to weddings didn't fit here. And I remember the first time I went to a formal dinner, one of those six-, seven-course dinners with all the forks and spoons. I was freaked! I didn't know what to do. I didn't finish a thing on my plate.

So you learn those kinds of things. Culturally, there was a lot of learning I had to catch up on. But I was trying not to be a *tío taco*, a sell-out. I needed to keep in touch with my friends who weren't going to college, because it's the worst thing in the world if you can't relate to the people you came up with. We have too many people in the Latino community who do that.

I was on a mission all through graduate school. I told everybody in graduate school, "I'm going back to East L.A. That's where they need me. That's where I come from." But I couldn't get any job offers there. L.A. is a little more racist, particularly within the decision-making structure. There is more fear of the Hispanic population because of the enormity of it. I couldn't penetrate that prejudice but it turned out that a hospital in San Jose was looking for somebody just like me, so I wound up accepting a job on the east side of San Jose working with *la comunidad latina*.

The hospital was right in the middle of the barrio in East San Jose, which is like East L.A. but on a much smaller scale. And it was under a lot of pressure from the Hispanic community to provide better service. A group of Hispanic organizations had even filed lawsuits against the hospital. I was brought in to do something about improving community relations, among other things.

The first thing I did was go out and talk with the community leaders. I sat down at the end of a rectangular table and met with representatives of eight or nine Hispanic organizations. And some of them were still out of the 1960s. A woman from La Raza Unida party said, "All, right, tell us about yourself, Señor Alvarez. Show us that your blood runs Latino."

It was okay, because I came from a Latino community and knew what was going on. But after six months of working with these community leaders, my boss called me in and said, "I want you to stop it."

"Am I doing something wrong?" I asked. "Well," he said, "you're going to make too many commitments, and these people are going to expect too much of us. You've got to stop."

"What commitments?" I said. "I'm not making any commitments. These people just want better service."

Finally, my boss got flustered with me and said, "Alvarez, you're never going to amount to anything if you continue to work with these people."

So I said, "Okay." I kept doing what I was doing, but I stopped telling him. If I had let him influence me, I wouldn't be successful today. He was one of the best examples of what I did not want to be.

═══════════════

OFF THE RECORD

If you say, "You racist son of a bitch," you're burning a bridge you may need to cross someday.

38-year-old senior marketing executive

MY last name is not Latino. I'm Mexican, but was adopted by an Anglo family. It's kind of funny at times, especially when I talk to people on the phone. It's an advantage and a disadvantage. Because if some people think they're talking with someone who is white, they'll say stuff they wouldn't say if they knew who I was. I've learned a lot of interesting things that way.

Once an interviewer said to me over the phone, "We've got this affirmative action spot, so I've got to find a Mexican." I said, "Guess what? You're in luck!"

Some people might think I'm a complete sell-out for not hanging up the phone. But there are ways of using anonymity to your advantage. I am the stealth Latina. I sneak in the door, and then they find out, "Oh, we hired one!"

The disadvantage is when some people who know who I am only on paper or on the phone finally meet me in person. They look at me and I can almost hear them say, "Oh, God, she's one of them!" If you say, "You racist son of a bitch," which is what you really want to say, you're burning a bridge you may need someday.

Actually, I've become more open-minded. I used to have this "they're all out to get me" feeling sometimes, which is hard not to have when you've heard and seen some of the things that I have. But I've sort of mellowed out and realize that well, none of us is perfect. We all have our biases. Some of them are more pernicious than others, but I'm going to try and put them aside.

═══════════════

I landed a position at IBM—and a head start on my career—because I could speak both English and Spanish.

Anthony Xavier Silva
Chairman and CEO
Corporate Systems Group

ONE thing we Hispanics need to do is develop our language skills so we can communicate effectively in English as well as in Spanish. In doing so, we remove the barriers of language restriction, thereby increasing our opportunities to succeed.

As Hispanics, I think we have a lot to be proud of. This country is not nearly as prejudiced against Hispanics as some people think. There's no question that many Hispanics don't get a fair break, and I wish that would change. However, if you can develop your language skills to communicate effectively and have a good rapport with Anglos as well as Hispanics, and anyone else you're dealing with, you'll be able to overcome some of the discrimination that is out there.

I had a bicultural upbringing. My parents spoke Spanish to each other and in turn would speak to me primarily in English. As a result I learned to speak English as well as many Anglos. My Spanish however, was very weak. In order to improve on this situation, when I reached the age of twelve, my parents decided to enroll me in a Jesuit Preparatory School in Little Havana. This was a total immersion experience, as more than 90 percent of the students and most of the faculty were Cuban-Americans. As a result, I was forced to adopt not only the Spanish language, but also my Cuban heritage throughout the next few years.

My career was launched when I was hired by IBM in 1985 after working at similar jobs for two other companies. IBM had a division at that time called NDD which sold IBM PC products in a professional retail environment. This division needed new employees who could speak Spanish, because they had a large contingent of Latin customers who did not speak English. Because of my previous job expriences and the fact that I was bilingual, they extended me a job offer. But I must confess that at the time, I somewhat exaggerated my ability to speak Spanish. While on the job, I quickly learned the basic PC vocabulary in Spanish, although I amused my Hispanic clients with my absolute butchering of the language. They thought, "This guy knows what he's talking about. He's just having a hard time translating into Spanish. Maybe I can help him." I got them so involved in helping me that they couldn't help but place an order!

The discrimination I've witnessed has largely occurred because people don't know I'm Hispanic. I've had them ask me when I'm traveling across the country, "What's it like in Miami with all those Cubans there? "Well," I say, "It's great. My folks are good people!" There's no point in getting angry. That doesn't help. It only reaffirms their foolish beliefs. They may not be worth wasting time on anyway.

INSIGHT 7

STAY ON TRACK

Personal and spiritual balance is the key to conquering obstacles and achieving success.

My father taught me it's easy for one knuckle-head to throw you off track, especially if you're a minority.

Mario Baeza
President
Wasserstein Perella International;
Chief Executive,
Latin American Operations
Wasserstein Perella & Company

MY parents came to this country, according to my father, so I would be born in the United States and would be eligible to become President. He also wanted me to speak Spanish. He was very much ahead of his time. He believed that while you're part of a group, and you should contribute and benefit from your closeness to that group, there's the whole world you have to conquer. You've got to be prepared in every way possible to participate. The double whammy was we were both black and Hispanic.

My father was a groundbreaker in a lot of ways. He grew up in Cuba, came here, went to college, graduated with honors from Cornell, got his BA and his master's, then went and got his Ph.D. from Michigan State. Meanwhile my mother was getting a master's in music from Columbia, which wasn't done back then. They were great role models for me.

Unfortunately, my father was born with congenital heart disease and died when I was fourteen. But not a day goes by that I don't think about him. And not a day goes by when I don't feel as though I directly benefit from the lessons he taught me.

My father would spend long hours after dinner smoking cigars, drinking cognac or brandy, and drilling me on hypothetical situations. "You'll be in this situation in your life someday," he'd say, "and this is what'll happen and this is the way you should play it."

"There'll be a time," my father once said, "when a good friend will pull up in front of the house with this shiny car and say, 'Come on in, take a ride.' And you'll think, 'Something's wrong with this picture. Where'd he get the car?' You've got to trust your instinct that if something doesn't look right, don't do it," he would say. "And the easy way out is to blame your father."

Sure enough the week after he died, my cousin pulled up in front of our house with this big car and said, "Come on, let's go for a ride." It played like a movie. I just heard my father's voice and I didn't get in the car. I made up some excuse. My cousin drove around the corner and got picked up by the police—stolen car, the whole nine yards.

My father told me about the time when he was at Cornell and ran into racist pressure. One of his professors was baiting him about a paper he had written. He had a great attitude, but he was being baited by this guy, until finally my father told him to take the paper and shove it up his ass and stormed out.

He called his father, my grandfather, and told him what had happened. My grandfather said, "Okay, now go apologize." The message: you can't let this knucklehead knock you off your whole life's path. You won't be able to graduate, and you get all screwed up because of this one knucklehead. You're going to run into knuckleheads all the time in life. So he went back and made peace with the guy.

My father's favorite phrase was "You've got to beat them at their own game." Which means you've got to understand the game, number one. Then you've got to figure out how to win.

OFF THE RECORD

It's important to understand that some people are never going to be your friend, not that you would ever want them as friends, and some of their attitudes just aren't going to change.

**43-year-old chief financial officer
of an agricultural products company**

SOMETIMES discrimination is very subtle, and when it's under the surface, it's almost more pernicious. Most people aren't going to come to you and say, "You dumb spic, you can't work on my deal." That would ring some bells. The challenge is the people who think it and are smart enough not to say it. It's very hard to ferret them out.

I've come across people who I thought were very "international" because they seemed interested in Latin American culture. It was an eye-opener when I realized that theirs was a *National Geographic* kind of interest. They loved going down and taking pictures of people in sombreros but in fact held Latinos in significant contempt.

I remember one person who said to me, "When I was in college I would take spring breaks in Cuba and it was a great time. I learned Spanish by watching some of the movies, and I remember smoking cigarettes at the Tropicana." To people like that, a visit to Latin America is like a combination of spending a day at a museum and a day at a zoo.

Things often come up in conversation as you are trying to build a relationship with some people and they let their guard down. For instance, they might say, "It's terrible to travel in Guatemala now. So many people are wearing jeans and cowboy boots instead of the traditional clothes that looked so picturesque. Now they just really want to be like everybody else in Texas." I've heard comments like that expressed in front of Mexicans in a business meeting. As my Mexican friends say to me, "Sometimes in these meetings we're viewed as Third World squirrels."

The real challenge is first, how are you going to contain people like that so their prejudices don't get in your way. And secondly, to what extent, personally and ethically, you can live with them. There are probably certain situations that come up where you have to draw the line and say no, this is just unacceptable. And given that behavior, I don't care if I make an enemy forever. You have to be able to take the consequences of your actions, one way or the other.

I try to divorce myself from overt prejudice, and I try to divorce the company from it. I'll make a semi-light comment: "Well, that is certainly an interesting anthropological view, but I'm sure it's not supported by anybody who's ever looked at the issue." But I also try to make it clear when I'm working for a client that ethnic remarks and slurs are just not acceptable. Then I come back here to the office, and tell other people here who I know would be as shocked as I am by what happened. Fortunately, there are enough of those people—and I think they're the vast majority—so that this person is, in effect, isolated. If only I make prejudice an issue, then it's easy for people to dismiss it and say, "Oh, he's a Latino. He's thin-skinned about this. He's just oversensitive."

OFF THE RECORD

Pride in yourself and your heritage is the best way to deal with prejudice.

48-year-old senior executive
of a manufacturing company

A guy made a crack about me at a company meeting. He was quoted in the minutes which I wasn't supposed to get. He said, "Who the hell does he think he is? Ain't no way in the world those boys from the south are going to let a Hispanic with black blood be president of this company."

I didn't really pay it any attention. The guy was an idiot. And he ultimately got the boot because of poor performance. But here was a case of someone actually saying what is on his mind. And for every time someone publicly says something like that, there are probably a thousand other people who are thinking, but never actually saying, racial slurs in the workplace.

What do you do about it? It happens, so be prepared. Be strong. Focus on the things you can change. Do the best job you can do and work with people who don't think this way.

Don't let someone else's prejudice become an interference.

Roman Martinez
Managing Director
Lehman Brothers

I'M very proud of my heritage and we speak Spanish at home. My kids spoke Spanish before they spoke English. But I am very proud of being an American. If you want to build a career, keep your focus on the professional aspect of it. Don't make your personal background or heritage an issue.

> *Don't think of yourself as underprivileged or disadvantaged or a victim. Think of yourself as a player.*

If you're going to try out for a football or a baseball team, more likely than not, you're going to make it because of what you can do in the field. Nobody's going to say, "You're black, so you must be be a good basketball player." Or, "You're Latin American so you must be a good short-

stop." That's not the way it is. The business world is similar.
   There are pockets of bigotry out there, and if you encounter it, don't let it become an interference. It's their
problem, not your problem. If they want to tackle you that
way, don't run into it, run around it. Be smarter.
   We all have a dimension that might be offensive to somebody. But don't be a fringe player because of that. Just go for
what interests you. And be the best at whatever job you're
doing. If you hit an obstacle, don't waste your time on it, figure out a way around it. Don't let it become a distraction.
You've got to make a judgment. Is it worth fighting or not?
What's the trade-off? Keep your eye on the ball.

===

*If you have a vision and believe in it enough,
other people will believe in it, too.*

Manuel D. Medina
President and CEO
Terremark Inc.

WHEN I was going to college I wanted to be a surfer, my hair
was real long, I had a hell of a tan, and I wore Salvation
Army surplus stuff. I had light hair and didn't "look Hispanic." I had a part-time job at a factory. Three Cuban ladies
also worked there, and from the moment I walked in, I
could tell they looked at me as a disgusting Americano.
   Right away they began making venomous remarks about
me to each other in Spanish: "Look at that kid. I bet you his
mother is a prostitute. I would boil his head in water and
take that hair off!" This went on for three or four days. Then
one day I came up behind one of the ladies, put my hand on
her back and said in Spanish, "So, do you think we're ever
going back to Cuba?"
   She dropped all her things! You should have seen the expression on her face.
   And you know what happened? All three ladies became

great friends of mine. They even cooked for me. I'll never ever forget that for the rest of my life. They probably will never forget it either!

The moral of the story: nobody is without prejudice— even Latinos.

If you're Latino, you should grab whatever opportunities you can and leverage them to the max. When you're just starting out, try to spend at least some time in an organization like a big bank, a big accounting firm, or a big law firm, because it teaches you a degree of excellence from the way you dress to the way you present a proposal that will stay with you forever.

Be prepared. Know your job, because there's nothing worse than confusing form for substance. Marketing people will tell you to wear a thousand-dollar suit and a custom-made shirt, even if they're the only ones you have. Fine. Once you get through the door you may look like a million bucks, but if you open your mouth and sound like a dollar, then people forget about what you look like. If you're Latino, if you're black, it doesn't matter. If you're the best, if you know what you're doing and you're good at it, you'll succeed. The toughest part is starting out. The important thing is not to quit.

Live up to your word. Anybody in this community I've ever done business with will tell you that if I give my word, I don't care what the papers say or the documents say, I'll live up to my word, even if it costs me money.

Create a reputation for keeping your word. If people know you're not going to screw them, they know they can trust you, then it doesn't matter whether you're Mexican, Cuban, or whatever.

Business can be very personal when you're working on your own or with a small company. It can be very impersonal when you're working in a big company. But still I believe that if you're good at what you do, persevere and create a reputation for keeping your word, then your heritage is not really going to play that big a part. If people have a problem with it, my advice is to ignore them. You know why? Because you can always use that as an excuse: "Oh, they don't like me because I'm this or that."

You know how lucky you are? Just think how dull your life would be if you were from just another cookie cutter and you were born in a pickup truck in North Carolina!

Manuel D. Medina is President and CEO of Terremark Inc., a Miami-based commercial real estate development firm. He came to the United States in 1965 when he was thirteen, graduated from Florida Atlantic University with an accounting degree, and started his career with Price Waterhouse in Florida. He has spearheaded many of Miami's most ambitious recent property developments, including the renewal of the Coconut Grove area, the CocoWalk retail complex, and the Brickell Bayfront Club.

Off the Record

Count to ten, don't take it too personally, and always relate it to the bottom line.

56-year-old entrepreneur and investor

You can't eliminate people's prejudices or racism overnight, but you can raise their sensitivity.

> *There are times when you have to fight prejudice by announcing clear ground rules and tying offensive behavior directly to business performance.*

A few years ago I developed a new project at a large entertainment company that was very innovative for the industry. We were about to launch it and it was going to get a lot of media attention. I had worked my butt off on this project and was very proud of what I had accomplished.

The president of my division was new to the job, and he had brought in a crony of his as head of marketing. They were golf buddies. Both of these guys were way overpaid and in way over their heads and everybody knew it. These guys then tried to hijack my project. They wanted to launch it their way—and take all the credit. Naturally, I resisted.

The division president called me into his office. He closed the door and began to swear, curse, and racially slur me at the top of his lungs, so loud that everyone else on the floor could hear.

I sat there calmly for about twenty minutes. Finally I asked him if he was finished and he said yes.

I then addressed all the criticisms he had made in a very calm, organized manner. Then I leaned forward and told him quietly that he was never, ever under any circumstances to address me in such a racist manner. And if he did, I would retaliate in a way that was decisive and, like his tirade, semi-public. Finally I told him that he was not going to hijack my project—there wasn't time to bring his crony up to speed, and if they launched the project their way, it would hurt the project and the company's bottom line.

These two guys backed off, the project got national attention, and was a huge success. This president never dared address me that way again.

Thanks to the project's success, I was recruited for a better job with another larger firm in the industry. The division president was fired a few months later.

Sometimes a bad boss comes with the territory.

Phil Ramos
CEO
Philatron International Inc.

THE second company I worked for was a good experience, I learned a lot, but it was also kind of a bad deal for me because I didn't like the philosophy of my boss. He was the type of guy who seemed a bit paranoid, who didn't trust his employees. He believed that he was more competent in every field. Well, you can't be an expert in everything.

When I was still new at the job, I went to discuss some things with him and he started to yell at me. I never would have imagined that an executive could act like that. But he was the owner of the company, and he just yelled and called me all kinds of names, and I walked out.

I was shocked and I felt like quitting, but I'm not a quitter. I said, "No, I made a commitment and I'm going to fulfill the job. Then I'll start my own company." And that's what I did. I'm a lot more mature now. If I was in that type of situation now, I don't think it would faze me. But then I was twenty-eight years old, and it really shook me up.

I would advise Latinos to remember that there will always be some people who will try to dominate and intimidate you. Some will do it by words, by yelling, by gestures. You've got to be aware of that and not let it shake you up.

Philip M. Ramos, Jr., is CEO of Philatron International Inc. in Santa Fe Springs, California, a $15 million annual revenue manufacturer of electronic and electrical cables, wires, and hose for automobiles and trucks. He was born into a Mexican-American family in Los Angeles, served in the Navy, earned a liberal arts degree from East Los Angeles College, and started Philatron with an initial investment of $168, working out of his garage. His firm has won awards for quality and service from General Dynamics, ITT, and Navistar.

Doors don't open easily. You've got to push them.

Richard Leza
President
AI Research Corporation

I learned many lessons from my *abuelo* in New Mexico. One summer we were working on a ranch, fixing fences, herding and branding cows. We had to get up at four in the morning and ride in a little truck heading up into the mountains. I always used to ride with my grandfather in the truck.

One time as we were riding along, he said, "Let me see your thumbs." I stuck out my thumbs and he grabbed them with his hands and asked me, "What are you going to do?"

"Well, I'm going to get out," I said. So I began to struggle and tried to get out but I couldn't do it. The more I tried, the more pressure he put on my thumbs until finally he let me go.

Then he told me, "The lesson of this game is that sometimes in life pressure is all around you and you really can't do anything about it. The problem is, the more you struggle the more pressure is going to be put on you. Try to look at the big picture and solve the problem without having to struggle. If you look me in the eyes, pretty soon I'm going to say, 'He's not struggling, he's not doing anything,' and I'm going to let you go."

> *You've got to be persistent, but in a way that applies your energy in the direction you want to go.*

A while back I went to some venture capital firms and said I'd like to get a job with them. "I've got everything you guys need," I told them. "I've got the experience, I've got the education." They were very polite, but they were very good at coming up with excuses. This was in 1981 and obviously they didn't feel comfortable with a Hispanic, so they weren't going to hire me. I don't care if people say it's got nothing to do with it. It's got a lot to do with it. They didn't feel comfortable with me. They wanted somebody with the same background, who looked like them, and had the same mentality.

I could have stopped right there and complained about it, but I remembered my grandfather's lesson about applying my energy in the direction I wanted to go. So I decided, "Well, if I can't do it directly, I'll try another way. Let's see if I can do some other things and get in through the back door."

That's when I started putting together deals for entrepreneurs and finding equity for them. I got involved in projects that venture capital firms weren't interested in doing. I got into the venture capital business through the "back door."

> *You can be discriminated against, but if you cry and complain about it too much, you're going to waste your energy on something that's not going to get you where you want to be in the future.*

I learned another valuable lesson from my mother. "A door will open if you put pressure on it," she once said. "They might want to keep it closed, but sooner or later if you keep pushing on it, they're going to get tired and you're going to open the door. Just keep up the pressure, and sooner or later it will open for you."

Richard L. Leza is President of AI Research Corporation of Mountain View, California, a venture capital firm investing in high-technology start-ups. He was born in Laredo, Texas, to a Mexican-American family, grew up in Hatch, New Mexico, and attended East Los Angeles College, New Mexico State University (BS in Civil Engineering), and the Stanford Graduate School of Business (MBA). He is the author of two books, *Develop Your Business Plan* and *Export Now,* and has established a fellowship for Hispanic students at the Stanford Graduate School of Business and a scholarship for Hispanic engineering students at New Mexico State University.

OFF THE RECORD

We need to focus more on supporting Latinos in positions of power, and less on bringing down the few who are there.

40-year-old CEO of a
professional services company

My worst day was when my ethics and integrity were falsely questioned by the Latino community. I have a position on the local Hispanic Chamber of Commerce and some people started saying I really didn't care about the community. I was truly offended. Then I thought, is this the Latino in me, this pride? Finally, I realized that people just might be envious of my position in the community. There will always be people who worry about their neighbor's backyard instead of their own. And jealousy is going to rise out of that.

> *Jealousy is one of the ugliest traits we can possess. And when it is directed at someone on the professional level, that's when snowballs grow into avalanches and rumors become dangerous.*

I decided to defend myself. I went out and faced the people who were accusing me. I said, "This is my position, this is my stand. I welcome your comments on issues that concern you about questions that have arisen." I laid it right on the table. I did nothing wrong. I told them I was totally committed to our community, and if they thought I was doing something wrong to come to me about it, not circulate rumors or question my integrity. I sat there and emphasized that "If you all would like to discuss anything, you can."

Rumors and jealousy are a part of everyday life in any community. Ever hear the story of the Mexican frogs? Two boys are fishing for frogs. When they're ready to break for lunch, they've got half a bucketful of frogs. And one boy says, "We can't leave. Those frogs are going to climb to the top and get out of the bucket." And the other boy says, "No, no, don't worry. Those are Mexican frogs. As soon as one frog starts climbing to the top, they'll all grab him by the leg and yank him back down."

When one Hispanic leader starts rising to the top and gains some credit and power, some other people think, "Hey, man, that should be me up there." They say, "Get back down here, you're nothing. Now I'm going to get to the top." I can't speak for other cultures, but I do know that in the Mexican culture, sometimes there's a perception of envy of people at the top. Or maybe it's just a part of the human formula that creates real problems for all of us when we have to deal with it.

═══════════════

You have to be an optimist.

Luis Lamela
CEO and President
CAC-United HealthCare Plans of Florida

I grew up in a family of eternal optimists. When we came to this country we had nothing. We lived in a shack on top of a converted garage. We used to brag to our mother about how good that was. "Look how lucky you are," we told her. "Some people have to clean houses that have three bedrooms. Here, all you have to do is turn on the fan and that pretty much takes care of the dirt!"

We've always been very, very positive, no matter what. For example, we all loved baseball. We didn't have money to buy tickets, so in the seventh inning, when the gates were opened and everybody was let in, our whole family would pile into the stadium and then pray for extra innings.

We'd go to a boat show or a car show, pose for pictures with our hands on brand-new boats and cars, then send them to friends and family back home and tell them, "Hey, it's great here in America!" Little did they know we were living in a shack.

I always used to tell my mother, "Just wait." I'd be walking with her, we'd see a beautiful car go by, and I'd say, "Mom, one day we're going to get that." And as it so happened, with a lot of hard work and even more optimism, we all eventually got where we wanted to go.

I don't hire pessimists.

Lionel Sosa
Chairman
DMB&B/Américas
Founder, Sosa, Bromley, Aguilar, Noble & Associates

WHEN people come into my office and start complaining about the last job they had and how wrong life has treated them, I escort them out of the office right away, because they tend to think that the world has done something bad to them.

I want people who are natural optimists, who just naturally see the bright side of things. I hire people with a sense of humor. If people are pessimists, I don't want to be near them. If they have a sense of humor and they are optimists, I want them around me.

OFF THE RECORD

Rejection can sometimes be great for your career.

53-year-old senior banking executive

SOME years ago, when I was working at a big bank in California, I was being considered for a promotion. The weekend before my interview with the personnel department I went to Squaw Valley to go skiing. It was a very sunny couple of days and I got really dark. I have a medium complexion.

I had the interview and I thought the personnel department liked me. But I didn't get the promotion. The personnel department decided that "this guy is pretty good, but we're not really sure he's the kind of guy that people will come in to borrow money from." I was judged as being "too dark and too Latin" to be a "credible" branch manager.

Now, obviously something like that could never ever be articulated today, but this was thirty years ago. And I found out about it three years later. Meanwhile, I had made a move into another department. And it turned out to be the best possible career option for me. I got in on the ground floor of the world of automation when computers in banking were still pretty new. And the opportunities that provided me were substantially greater than they would have been if I'd stayed in branch banking.

Control is an illusion.

Jose Rivero
President
Praxair Canada

SOME of us are always trying to be in control of things—in control of what's happening today, in control of the future.

You can never be in complete control. You do the best you can and generally hope that the actions you're taking are correct and aimed in the right direction. But to really believe you have control over everything that's going to happen is a big mistake.

I had the pleasure of listening to Colin Powell at a forum in Orlando not so long ago. He was very impressive. He was talking about things that he looks for in people—integrity and loyalty, but most importantly "the ability to corner." He said when he turns a corner quickly, he wants to be sure that when he looks over he sees his wing man is still there.

> *Events that you predict are going to happen, may not, and probably more likely will not. So your ability to notice when they do not and to adjust, to corner quickly, will be the key to success in today's business environment.*

Things are changing very rapidly in every business today. Set forth in the direction you believe is right, but constantly be on the lookout for opportunities you can take advantage of or mistakes you may have made.

And then corner. Corner quickly.

Jose Rivero is Vice President of Praxair, Inc. and President of Praxair Canada, a wholly owned subsidiary company. Praxair, Inc. is the largest industrial gases supplier in North and South America. Mr. Rivero holds a bachelor of science degree in aerospace engineering and a master of engineering degree, both from the University of Florida.

OFF THE RECORD

Latinos shouldn't expect special treatment, but we should expect not to be treated as if we are all alike.

38-year-old telecommunications
company executive

WHEN I started my career back in 1978, there was still a lot of the civil rights push from the 1960s and the early 1970s. I thought there would have been greater emphasis on being recognized as a Latino or other minority, and getting opportunities because of that. In fact, I didn't find that to be the case at all.

> *You may get a foot in the door because you're a minority, but I don't think it makes a significant difference in terms of your overall opportunities for promotion. You still have to fit into the organization, and you still have to deliver results.*

You cannot assume that just because you're a Latino that you're going to get special preference. They may give you a break, but you've still got to prove yourself.

There's also a tremendous amount of ignorance even today about Latinos. It's assumed that people with Spanish surnames are all alike. In fact, the heritage of someone born in Chile is substantially different from my heritage. And there are significant cultural differences among Latinos, depending on where they were born and brought up. I'm not saying they're good or bad. They're just different.

Live the moment but give time a chance.

Tony Bustamante
Executive Vice President, Chief Trader
HSBC Markets, division of Midland Bank plc

YOU have to take advantage of the moment. You have to live the moment.

When I was growing up I learned how, instead of having

to spend money to get new soles when you had a hole in your shoes, you could take the top of a little can of condensed milk, tap it around so you didn't cut yourself, and put in between the leather so the water wouldn't go in. I lived all those years as if they were an adventure. I never worried about the landlady coming to collect the rent. I knew I had to pay and I did the best I could to pay. I knew that in time, with hard work, I would overcome all these obstacles.

When I first started out in business, I was a junior guy working in a trading room at the Bank of New York in a very junior position and I met this gentleman who asked me, "Are you good with numbers?" I said, "I'm the best there is with numbers."

"Well, why don't you come work for me in the foreign exchange department," he said. "If you can learn this business, you're going to do very well because there's a great future in it."

I took his word for it. He was the head of the foreign exchange department. Now I am. He taught me the business. And I've been with the same bank since 1972.

> *You have to take advantage of the moment, of an opportunity if it's offered. Most of all, if you try a little bit harder than the guy next to you, in this country you can succeed.*

But you also have to have patience. Sometimes people expect too much of themselves and of the company they work for. I realize that you can only have so much patience. But you have to prove yourself over time.

Tony Bustamante is Executive Vice President and Chief Trader at HSBC Markets, a division of Midland Bank plc in New York City. He grew up in Cuba, Miami, and New York, and started his career at the Bank of New York as a trainee. He often lectures on the subject of foreign exchange and international finance.

OFF THE RECORD

Your family should have a higher priority than your career.

40-year-old consumer products
marketing executive

YOU'VE got to talk to your spouse about what really matters most to *both* of you. I've seen a lot of colleagues work hard to achieve bigger career advancements than they ever dreamed of. But in the process they seriously damaged their health and their marriages. In the end they were very successful career-wise, but they had nobody to share it with.

My godmother is eighty years old and is still working on the family farm. Every time I go back there, she says, The heck with your title, what are you getting out of life?

She cuts right to the key issue. "Don't forget the fundamentals in life," she says. "You work too hard, you travel too much, you don't see enough of the people you care about—and we are all going to end up in the same box, whether you're vice president or not."

> *If all you're shooting for in life is a job title or a certain salary, you'll be disappointed even if you get them. If you don't have the other important things in life, you're going to feel empty-handed. In today's world no company will give you the lifetime satisfaction you get from a family.*

A colleague of mine was fired when he was a company president in his forties. He was devastated because his whole life was wrapped up in his career and now he had nothing else. His entire self-esteem depended on his title and what he did at work, and he even enjoyed his job. But if you put all your eggs in one basket, that's a risky proposition. *Balance* is important.

I see the stress that my current travel schedule puts on my marriage. And there's a certain point where I draw a line. I have shareholders too, and my shareholders are my wife, myself, and my health.

My family has been important to me since day one. I attribute that to my culture. I once had to turn down a job offered to me by the head of my company because it involved a move my wife and I were not ready for. I said to one of my closest friends in the company, "If he makes it a make-or-break issue, I'm willing to get fired over this." I knew my career meant a lot to me, but I wouldn't give up my marriage for it. I wasn't going to screw up what matters most.

When I turned the job down, it was a very emotional issue for me. I was thinking, boy, I may have just shot myself in the foot. But I didn't feel guilty, because I was doing the right thing for what matters most—my family.

The boss heard me out and then said, "You've got your head in the right place. This is not a bullet that will end your career. You have the knowledge and diversity of experience. Things will work out over the long term. You'll get other opportunities."

I came home that night feeling very good about myself. A lot of other people would've been afraid even to have a discussion like that. They would've thought, hell, he's going to fire me if I don't take the job, so I'll do what I have to do. I made the right decision. If I hadn't, I would have regretted it the rest of my life.

You are always more effective not just by working harder, but by bringing balance to your life.

Enrique Guardia
Group Vice President
Kraft General Foods USA

I was sent to Brussels to head up research and development for all of Europe at a time when my company was having troubles. We were all working very hard. I was so focused on the company that I was probably short-sheeting my family. Then my wife became very ill and all of a sudden I saw the whole company situation from a very different perspective. It was not the end of the world. My wife being ill could have been the end of the world.

Illness in the family is never fun, but when you're ill overseas it's all that much more complicated. So I went to my boss and said, "My wife is ill and I've got to stop traveling." I thought he was going to fire me. He didn't.

At times we lose balance in our lives. I had taken my whole family situation for granted. So the profound lesson I learned, although I hope other people don't have to learn it the same way, was that it's the balance you bring to your life and your work that really count. If you sacrifice your family to your work, you're not traveling on the right road.

It's not always easy to achieve balance in jobs that demand more and more of us. But you've got to listen to your conscience and listen to your family. I came home one night and my son said, "I played a Ping-Pong match and won. I was the best in my class and you weren't even there." That hit me deeply and profoundly.

In many Hispanic homes, not only are you taking care of your spouse and kids, but your parents as well. When things get tough, some people try to be heroes and continue meeting the demands of work for the fear of losing their jobs. Again, it's important to find the right balance. And don't be afraid to ask for help.

═══════════

If who you are determines where your company will send you, it's time to leave that company.

Adela Cepeda
President and Founder
AC Advisory

ABOUT two years before I left the large investment bank I was working for, something happened that confirmed my decision that I had to leave. I was working on a very complicated assignment. A Michigan company was undergoing a major reorganization involving certain tax issues. I became an expert on the assignment. The company reorganized and then had to sell one of its divisions. I searched all over the world for someone interested in buying this division. Finally we found somebody in England, and the chairman of the Michigan company was going to go to England to meet with this company.

I assumed that either my boss would go, or I would go, since I knew everything about the transaction. But as it was getting near the time for the trip, my boss told me, "No, you aren't going. We have to send Joe from the mergers and acquisitions department."

"You're going to send who?" I said. "He's twenty-five years old. He barely knows anything about the transaction." "The chairman would never feel comfortable with you," my boss said. "What do you mean?" I said. "Well, I just don't think it would work," he said.

I was devastated. And it suddenly hit me that the things that made my client uncomfortable were things I could not change—my ethnic background and gender. I was furious because I had worked for that client. It was a very painful experience, and really the first time that I ever felt discrimination against me. Some people talk about supporting minorities and women in management but don't put their money behind it.

When I left that bank in 1991 and started my own business, it felt like a major release because my business is women-owned and minority-controlled. Maybe I couldn't change the things that seemed to make some people uncomfortable, but I could certainly change jobs.

═══════════

If you really want to crack that glass ceiling, you can start your own company.

Maria Elena Toraño
Founder, Chairman, and CEO
META Inc.

I'VE come up against the "double glass ceiling." I'm a double minority—a Hispanic and a woman.

How do you overcome obstacles? You go through life building blocks, or putting blocks in place. Those blocks are knowledge, skill, and experience. You may go through long stretches where all you do is work hard. But if you're building blocks of knowledge, skill, and experience, suddenly you turn those blocks into steps and you climb quite fast. In life you must "pay your dues." Then when the opportunity for a promotion, a better job, or even starting your own company comes along, you're more than ready to take it on and get the support needed to succeed.

Maria Elena Toraño is Founder, Chairman, and CEO of META Inc., a management consulting company based in Miami and Washington, D.C. She was born in Havana, received a bachelor's degree from the University of Havana, began working in the mailroom of the Aetna Life Insurance Company in Miami, and held management positions at Eastern Air Lines in Miami and Puerto Rico. She also served as a high school teacher, welfare supervisor, and hospital administrator. In 1979 she founded META, which now has has over $20 million in sales and a staff of three hundred. She is the founder of the National Hispanic Leadership Institute.

OFF THE RECORD

Discrimination happens not only in the United States but all throughout the world. Learn to overcome it. Look at it in a practical way.

50-year-old broadcasting executive

ONE thing that can be very detrimental and negative to Latinos is the sense that some people have that we are second-class citizens.

I came to this country with a degree of education, understanding, and general knowledge, but because I didn't know the language, in many instances I felt—I don't want to say discriminated against—but not really seen for who I was and what I was able to do. But I've come to realize that there's a certain degree of discrimination everywhere. People are going to discriminate against you not only because of your background, but because of your religion, your color, whatever. It happens, no matter where you are.

Discrimination is there, and some people dwell on it and allow that negativity to drag them down. If they don't succeed in their lives, it's because they were discriminated against. But I've been very careful to deal with it in a very pragmatic way.

Years ago, a couple of young friends and I went to look at an apartment in Newark, New Jersey. We rang the bell and a woman came out, took one look at us and said, "I'm sorry, I don't rent to Hispanics." That was in 1964. We were insulted and walked away. We didn't know we had any legal recourse. But I didn't dwell on the experience. And we eventually found a much better apartment.

======

A therapist is like a dentist but for a different purpose. Latinos need to understand that.

Jim Saavedra
Senior Vice President
Union Bank

I was once hired by a guy who used to work for me. There was a little bit of an ego blow there. And quite frankly, it was a step backward from a career standpoint, which added emotional issues to the situation. I had this huge anxiety attack about three weeks into the job and I didn't know what was wrong with me.

I went and talked to a counselor, a therapist. And in talking to him it suddenly occurred to me that I thought there was a possibility that I might fail in a step I had already progressed beyond. That was what was causing my anxiety.

The principal role of a therapist is to be a very good full-length mirror to help you to see what you can't see even though it's right there in front of you. You know something's going on, but you can't tell what it is. We all need help at some point. Going to a therapist is like going to a dentist when you've got a toothache. Latinos should understand that. Simply understanding what was going on and what was scaring me was personally very freeing for me. But for many Latinos it can be hard to seek help like that. I credit my wife for encouraging me.

It's not just typical of Latinos. I think a lot of minorities have a reluctance to seek help. The first thing you focus on is being different. And if you focus too much on being different, it is very difficult to see that you're not. A lot of what we go through is very normal. But we're afraid to let it be seen. And because we're afraid to let it be seen, we never get beyond it.

Don't be afraid to say, "This is not for me."

Emilio Alvarez-Recio
Vice President, Global Advertising
Colgate-Palmolive Company

DON'T spend one second of your life pursuing something you find painful in any way other than the pain caused by hard work. If you're doing something you don't like, you're not going to be very good at it, and you're going to be incredibly unhappy in your life.

I never really remember thinking somebody had a problem with me because I was Hispanic or I was brown. I always figured it was because I was kind of short and ugly!

Andy Plata
Founder and CEO
COPI- Computer Output Printing Inc.

I was reared in San Antonio, Texas. My mom was determined that I would get a higher education and amount to something. It became grafted on me even when I didn't realize it. As other kids were being rocked to sleep with lullabies, my mom was singing, "You'll go to college, you'll go to college . . . " Before I was even conscious of it, she was putting that expectation into my brain.

I went to what I call a two-door high school. One door was for the non-Anglos, mostly Chicanos, and the other was for the fairly wealthy Anglos. I started hanging around with the wrong people and ended up in a gang. It wasn't like gangs are today, but was still not a good situation. Friends of mine were injured, shot, beat up, things like that, so it was a pretty intense time. Actually, some positive things came from the gang experience. I learned how to organize people and provide them with resources. These were some of the same skills that helped me succeed later in mainstream business situations.

After graduation a friend of mine and I, who were the leaders of the gang, went to California. Our goal was to become Hell's Angels, so we hung out on Sunset Strip. The Hell's Angels eventually came up. They wouldn't even talk to us. So you see, I'm a rejected Hell's Angel. Actually, I was ignored, which I guess is worse than rejection! That was probably my first experience of total discrimination. We were discriminated against by the Hell's Angels because either we weren't dirty enough or we weren't the right color. Whatever the reason, we didn't qualify.

My parents really never gave me much information about being discriminated against. I figured I was discriminated against because I was such an animal, the way I looked and dressed. Today, if someone came in my house looking the way I did back then, I don't care who they are, they'd be discriminated against.

So I didn't grow up looking for people to discriminate against me. I really didn't see much of it. But I do know that after I founded my own company, discrimination affected how we ran it.

One time a customer called us and said, "Look, you need to assign somebody else to my account." I said, "Why is that?" And he said, "Well, I just don't like dealing with women."

"Well," I said, "Let me think about this and call you back." I called him back and said, "Here's the problem. If I assign somebody else to your account, what happens if they're black or Mexican like me. One of the things I'd like to do is find a way for you to judge the person you're dealing with by their ability." He didn't like that answer. He left us as a customer and went to a competitor. Eight months later he was bankrupt and left the competitor with a large unpaid invoice.

One of the challenges we seem to have in the Latino culture is this macho thing. And that needs to be gotten rid of. Today, most of COPI's business is done in strategic alliances with other companies and a lot of my time is spent helping the companies we work with get away from macho attitudes.

For example, we own a company that does maintenance on printers around the country and I got a call from one of our customers who said, "This is terrible. Your people aren't getting the work done." I flew some people in to fix the problem. Then I sat down with our people to review the situation. "Why didn't I know about this?" I asked the guy in charge. "And number two, if you had a problem, why didn't you ask for help?" It was the macho thing. People up and down the line didn't want to admit they had a problem bigger than what they could figure out. They didn't want to take the chance that somebody would think they didn't know it all.

If we go around telling people that we know it all, nobody is invited to help us. Pride is good. But excessive and destructive pride is what keeps us from succeeding to our maximum potential. We have to be more open, more vulnerable. Vulnerability means letting go of destructive pride.

I read in Scripture that the meek shall inherit the earth. I couldn't understand what that meant since I thought the meek were the people who just sat around doing nothing. Then I learned what it really meant was that the people who will succeed are the people who are humble and meek enough to be vulnerable. This vulnerability allows them to hear advice from others, to improve and succeed.

Don't forget to do some spiritual exercise.

Phil Ramos
CEO
Philatron International Inc.

As a tournament tennis player, I'm always trying to stay in physical shape, but there's also spiritual exercise. I'll start out the day by reading two chapters of the Bible. Spiritual exercise, I believe, is what gives me the strength to get through adverse situations. I don't get so shook up anymore. If I'm facing a critical situation, I'm very confident because I have that spirit in me. I'm a Christian Catholic and I feel close to Jesus. I just feel that I'm doing what's right. And I'm honest.

I recommend to young Latinos that they don't forget to do some spiritual exercise, like praying and reading the Bible. I get a lot of insights from the Bible. Both the Old Testament and the New Testament teach you how to deal with your fellow man. And that really helps me quite a bit in my business. I've often thought that Jesus would be a great business manager. He was a role model, he was honest, he taught. He gave course correction and feedback. He was demanding. And he expected good things from people.

We must serve as an army of role models.

Carlos H. Cantu
President and CEO
The ServiceMaster Company

THE ultimate measure of your success will depend on your personal achievement, self-reliance, and spiritual development. As Latinos, we must also serve as an army of mentors to those in our community who may be stuck in the cycle of failure and poverty.

> *We have a fundamental moral obligation to help each other, and while some of us may rise faster than others, our ultimate goal should be that we all rise together, while maintaining our individuality.*

We should be on guard against those groups or organizations that may seek to isolate us in the erroneous belief that only through isolation can our culture and heritage survive. It's not enough to insist on "our share of the pie." It's even more important to demand our share of responsibility and accountability.

Carlos H. Cantu is President and CEO of the The ServiceMaster Company in Downers Grove, Illinois, a $2.9 billion company specializing in lawn care, pest control, and home services and facilities management. He was born in Brownsville, Texas, and started his career with a Mexican agricultural products company. In 1970 he went to work for Terminix, and within eight years was president of the company. After Terminix was acquired by ServiceMaster in 1986, he rose to become President and CEO of ServiceMaster.

It's so important that we stress education to other Latinos.

> Marcos Avila
> **President**
> **Cristina Saralegui Enterprises**

IT'S a tremendous problem, the education problem. So many of our kids are dropping out of high school and setting themselves up for failure. Many of our people coming up in the barrio don't have any expectations. What expectations do they have? The boys are expected to do wrong, the girls are expected to be pregnant by fourteen. It's a terrible vicious circle. Successful Latinos have to get involved and help these people out.

Montgomery Ward wanted to sign Cristina on as a spokesperson, and we said, "Okay, but what are you guys doing for Hispanics? What are you guys doing to help out some of the same customers that you have that you're making a living from?" As a result, they created a Hispanic Scholarship Fund.

In order to receive, you have to give.

Gary Trujillo
President and CEO
The Southwest Harvard Group Companies

I was not "supposed" to succeed.

I was a kid from the barrio of South Phoenix, a very low-income environment. I grew up with mariachi music and Mexican food. My parents lived in a house they bought thirty-five years ago with a $6,000 mortgage.

After I graduated from college, I worked on Wall Street for several years and then went to Harvard Business School. In the summer of 1990 I called my best friend, Jesus Valenzuela, who was then the youngest CFO that Gerber Foods International had ever had. He and I had met at Arizona State University. I said, "Hey, remember the dreams we had back in college to start a business? Well, I'm going to do it, and I want you to do it with me."

We bought a little real estate company here in Phoenix that was kind of a mom-and-pop shop. It was owned by another Mexicano, and we took it from being a $200,000 company by the end of the first year to being a $1 million company. It cost us $50,000. Jess put up $25,000 and I put up $25,000. And at that point I was still $80,000 in debt to Harvard Business School.

I remember the day we bought the company. It was on a Sunday when we finally signed all the documents. We believed it was fate and we were being guided by a stronger force. So we all went to church that Sunday, and after the Mass, we asked the priest to bless us and the agreements before we signed them.

We went from having five employees in 1990 to having over four hundred employees today. It wasn't without hard work, but our success was largely due to our respecting and appreciating others. In business you have many opportunities to take advantage of people, and we have always been committed to making sure that we dealt with everyone in good faith.

My goal is to achieve a consistent cash flow that will help me achieve a good standard of living, but more importantly that will help me give back to the community I grew up in. The one thing I've learned is that it's critical to give back. I'm a mentor to a lot of young kids right now. That's because when I was young, people took me under their wing. And I'm trying to do the same because you receive the greatest return on life when you give of yourself.

Gary Trujillo is President and CEO of The Southwest Harvard Group Companies of Phoenix, Arizona, an asset management and investment company. He was born and raised in Phoenix, graduated from Arizona State University, and spent six years on Wall Street working in sales, trading, and public finance for Salomon Brothers. He then earned an MBA at Harvard Business School. A business school field study he performed evolved into a business plan for the company he launched in 1990 with his partner, Jesus Valenzuela.

THE 100 BEST COMPANIES FOR LATINOS

The following list of the 100 best companies in the U.S. offering the greatest job and career opportunities for Latinos is reprinted with the cooperation of *Hispanic* magazine, which conducted a national survey with several hundred major companies.

Four areas were evaluated: 1. recruitment and hiring; 2. education; 3. minority vendor programs; and 4. support for Hispanic organizations. The analysis was qualitative as well as quantitative. For example, a company with few Hispanics in top management may nonetheless have an active minority vendor program. Also, consideration was given to what a company is trying to achieve, as well as what has actually been achieved. Nowhere is it more true than in corporate America that you must walk before you can run.

The decision to limit the list to 100 top companies was certain to invite disappointments. Some irate executives called to complain about their companies' being excluded. In each case, the decision was somewhat different. Many otherwise outstanding corporations continue to have a blind spot when it comes to the Hispanic community. While many companies boast about their support for minorities, when you ask a few tough questions, a different story emerges. For example, how many Hispanics serve on the board of directors? How many are in top management? A

number of companies are justly proud of their support for
the African-American community but forget that Hispanics
are also entering the workforce in large numbers. But we
are proud to include the *Hispanic* magazine list of "The 100
Companies Providing the Most Opportunities for Hispanics," and we offer our special thanks to Andres Cordero for
his fine efforts in compiling this report.

AFLAC
1932 Wynnton Road
Columbus, GA 31999
706-323-3431

Allstate
2775 Sanders Road
Northbrook, IL 60062-6127
708-402-5000

American Airlines
Dallas/Fort Worth Airport
TX 75261-9616
817-963-1234

American Express
200 Vesey Street
New York, NY 10285
212-640-2000

Ameritech
30 South Wacker
Chicago, IL 60606
312-727-9411

Anheuser-Busch
One Busch Place
St. Louis, MO 63118
314-577-2000

Apple Computer
One Infinite Loop
Cupertino, CA 95014
408-996-1010

ARCO
515 South Flower Street
Los Angeles, CA 90071
213-486-3511

AT&T
32 Avenue of the Americas
New York, NY 10013-2412
201-387-5400

Avon
9 West 57th Street
New York, NY 10019
212-546-6015

Bank of America
Bank of America Center
555 California Street
San Francisco, CA 94104
415-622-3456

Bank One
100 E. Broad Street
Columbus, OH 43271
614-248-5944

Baxter Healthcare
One Baxter Parkway
Deerfield, IL 60015
708-948-2000

BellSouth
1155 Peachtree Street, NE
Atlanta, GA 30309-3610
404-249-2000

Boeing
P. O. Box 3707
Seattle, WA 98124-2207
206-655-2121

Borden
180 East Broad Street
Columbus, OH 43215-3799
614-225-4000

Bristol-Myers Squibb
345 Park Avenue
New York, NY 10154-0037
212-546-4000

Chase Manhattan
One Chase Manhattan Plaza
New York, NY 10081-0001
212-552-2222

Chevron Corporation
575 Market Street
San Francisco, CA 94105
415-894-7700

Chrysler Corporation
800 Chrysler Drive East
Auburn Hills, MI
  48326
313-956-5741

Chubb
15 Mountain View Road
Warren, NJ 07059
908-903-2000

Citibank
399 Park Avenue
New York, NY 10043
212-559-1000

Coca-Cola
One Coca-Cola Plaza
Atlanta, GA 30301
404-676-2121

Colgate-Palmolive
300 Park Avenue
New York, NY 10022-7499
212-310-2000

Compaq Computer
P. O. Box 692000
Houston, TX 77269-2000
713-370-0670

Consolidated Edison
  of New York, Inc.
4 Irving Place
New York, NY 10003
212-460-4600

Coors Brewing
311 Tenth Street
NH475
Golden, CO 80401-0030
800-642-6116

Delta Airlines
1030 Delta Boulevard
Atlanta, GA 30320
404-715-2600

Diamond Shamrock
9830 Collonade Blvd.
San Antonio, TX 78230
210-641-6800

DuPont
1007 Market Street
Wilmington, DE 19898
302-774-1000

Eastman Kodak
343 State Street
Rochester, NY 14650
716-724-4000

EDS
5400 Legacy Drive
Plano, TX 75024
214-604-6000

Eli Lilly
Lilly Corporate Center
Indianapolis, IN 46285
317-276-2000

Exxon
800 Bell Street
Houston, TX 77002-7426
713-656-3636

Federal Express
P. O. Box 727
Memphis, TN 38194
901-369-3600

First Union Bank
225 Water Street
Jacksonville, FL 32202
904-361-2265

Ford
The American Road
Dearborn, MI 48121-1899
313-322-3000

General Electric
3135 Easton Turnpike
Fairfield, CT 06431
203-373-2211

General Motors
3044 West Grand Boulevard
Detroit, MI 48202
313-556-5000

Gillette
1 Gillette Park
South Boston, MA 02127
617-421-7000

Goya Foods
100 Seaview Drive
Secaucus, NJ 07096
201-348-4900

Hallmark
2501 McGee Street
Kansas City, MO 64108
816-274-5111

Hoechst Celanese
1041 Route 202/206
Somerville, NJ 08876-1258
908-231-2000

Home Savings of America
4900 Rivergrade Road
Irwindale, CA 91706
818-960-6311

Honda
1919 Torrance Boulevard
Torrance, CA 90501
310-783-2000

Honeywell
Honeywell Plaza
Minneapolis, MN 55440
612-951-1000

IBM
20 Old Post Road
Armonk, NY 10504
914-765-2000

ITT
1330 Avenue of the Americas
New York, NY 10019-5490
212-258-1000

JCPenney
6501 Legacy Drive
P.O. Box 10001
Dallas, TX 75301
214-431-0000

Johnson & Johnson
One Johnson & Johnson
    Plaza
New Brunswick, NJ 08933
908-524-0400

Kaiser Permanente
One Kaiser Plaza
Oakland, CA 94612
510-271-5910

Kellogg
One Kellogg Square
Battle Creek, MI 49016
616-961-2000

Kraft
Three Lakes Drive
Northfield, IL 60093
708-646-2000

Kroger
16770 Imperial Valley
    Drive
Houston, TX 77060
713-507-4800

Lockheed Martin
6801 Rockledge
    Drive
Bethesda, MD 20817
301-897-6000

McDonald's
One Kroc Drive
Oakbrook, IL 60521
708-575-3000

MCI
1801 Pennsylvania Avenue,
    NW
Washington, DC 20006
202-872-1600

MetLife
One Madison Avenue
New York, NY 10010
212-578-2211

Miller Brewing
3939 West Highland
    Boulevard
Milwaukee, WI 53208
414-931-2000

Mobil
3225 Gallows Road
Fairfax, VA 22037
703-846-3000

Motorola
1303 E. Algonquin Road
Schaumburg, IL 60196
708-576-5000

NationsBank
NationsBank Center
100 North Tryon Street
Charlotte, NC 28255-0001
704-386-5000

Nestlé USA
800 North Brand Boulevard
Glendale, CA 91203
818-549-6000

New York Life
51 Madison Avenue
New York, NY 10010
212-576-5151

New York Times
229 W. 43rd Street
New York, NY 10036
212-556-1234

Nike
One Bowerman Drive
Beaverton, OR 97005-6453
503-671-6453

Nissan
18501 S. Figueroa
Carson, CA 90248-4500
310-532-3111

Nordstrom
1501 Fifth Avenue
Seattle, WA 98101-1603
206-628-2111

NYNEX
1095 Avenue of the Americas
New York, NY 10036
212-395-2121

Pacific Bell
130 Kearny Street
San Francisco, CA 94108
415-394-3000

Pacific Gas and Electric
77 Beale Street
San Francisco, CA 94105
415-973-7000

PepsiCo
700 Anderson Hill Road
Purchase, NY 10577
914-253-2000

Pfizer
235 E. 42nd Street
New York, NY 10017-5755
212-573-2323

Philip Morris
120 Park Avenue
New York, NY 10017
212-880-5000

Procter & Gamble
One Procter & Gamble Plaza
Cincinnati, OH 45202
513-983-1100

Prudential
751 Broad Street
Newark, NJ 07102-3777
201-802-6000

Rockwell
2201 Seal Beach Boulevard
Seal Beach, CA 90740-8250
310-797-3311

Ryder
3600 N.W. 82nd Avenue
Miami, FL 33166
305-593-3726

Sathers
Sathers Round Lake
One Sathers Plaza
Round Lake, MN 56167-0028
800-533-0330

SBC Communications
175 East Houston
San Antonio, TX 78205
210-351-2158

Schieffelin & Somerset
Two Park Avenue
New York, NY 10016
212-251-8200

Seagram
375 Park Avenue
New York, NY 10152
212-572-7000

Sears
3333 Beverly Road
Hoffman Estates, IL 60179
708-286-2500

Shell
910 Louisiana Street
Houston, TX 77002
713-241-6161

Smithkline Beecham
One Franklin Plaza
200 N. 16th Street
Philadelphia, PA 19102
800-366-8900

Southland
2711 North Haskell Avenue
Dallas, TX 75204
214-828-7011

Southwest Airlines
2702 Love Field Drive
Dallas, TX 75235
214-904-4000

Sprint
2330 Shawnee Mission
  Parkway
Westwood, KS 66205
913-624-3000

State Farm
One State Farm Plaza
Bloomington, IL 61710
309-766-2311

Sun Microsystems
2550 Garcia Avenue
Mountain View, CA 94043-
  1100
415-960-1300

Texaco
P. O. Box 1404
Houston, TX 77251-1404
713-666-8000

Texas Instruments
13500 N. Central Expressway
Dallas, TX 75243
214-995-2551

Time Warner
75 Rockefeller Plaza
New York, NY 10019
212-484-8000

Toyota
19001 South Western Avenue
Torrance, CA 90509
310-618-4000

TRW Space and Electronics
  Group
One Space Park
Redondo Beach, CA 90278
310-812-4321

U S WEST
7800 East Orchard Road
Englewood, CO 80111
303-793-6500

United Airlines
1200 Algonquin Road
Elk Grove Township, IL 60007
708-952-4000

Wells Fargo Bank
420 Montgomery Street
San Francisco, CA 94104
415-396-3053

WMX Technologies
3003 Butterfield Road
Oak Brook, IL 60521
708-572-8800

Xerox
800 Long Ridge Road
Stamford, CT 06904
203-968-3000

INDEX TO BIOGRAPHIES

Dear *Latino Success* Readers:

We'd love to hear from you! Send your comments or just your address if you would like to be included in our mailings to:

TropiX Media, Inc.
P.O. Box 1741
Murray Hill Station
New York, NY 10156
or by e-mail to: TropiXinc@AOL.com

ABOUT THE AUTHORS

Augusto Failde is President of TropiX Media, Inc., a New York firm that creates new media ventures and programming for Latino markets in the United States and Latin America. He is currently launching Latino Entertainment Television (LTV), the first cable television network devoted to bilingual and English-speaking Latinos. He helped develop and launch several new cable networks, including *HBO en Español, ESPN Latin America,* and *Fox Latin America.* He holds a BA from Stanford University and an MBA from Harvard Business School. He lives in New York City.

William Doyle is a New York-based writer and has held management positions at J. Walter Thompson and Time Warner.